COLOR, CLASS,
AND PERSONALITY

MEMBERS OF
THE AMERICAN YOUTH COMMISSION

Appointed by the American Council on Education

OWEN D. YOUNG, New York
Chairman

HENRY I. HARRIMAN, Boston
Vice Chairman

MIRIAM VAN WATERS, Framingham, Massachusetts
Secretary

WILL W. ALEXANDER, Chicago

CLARENCE A. DYKSTRA, Madison

DOROTHY CANFIELD FISHER, Arlington, Vermont

WILLARD E. GIVENS, Washington

GEORGE JOHNSON, Washington

MORDECAI W. JOHNSON, Washington

CHESTER H. ROWELL, San Francisco

WILLIAM F. RUSSELL, New York

JOHN W. STUDEBAKER, Washington

HENRY C. TAYLOR, Chicago

MATTHEW WOLL, New York

GEORGE F. ZOOK, Washington

FLOYD W. REEVES, *Director*

COLOR, CLASS, AND PERSONALITY

BY ROBERT L. SUTHERLAND

Prepared for
The American Youth Commission

AMERICAN COUNCIL ON EDUCATION
Washington, D.C., 1942

COPYRIGHT 1942 BY THE AMERICAN COUNCIL ON EDUCATION
WASHINGTON, D.C.   PUBLISHED JANUARY 1942

> Brief parts of this report may be quoted without special permission provided appropriate credit is given. Permission to quote extended passages may be secured through the American Council on Education, 744 Jackson Place, Washington, D.C.

305.896073
S966c

All the names of persons used in the case study and interview materials in this book are pseudonyms.

FOREWORD

SPECIAL DISADVANTAGES are faced by a tenth of American youth between 16 and 24 years of age—the two and a quarter million Negroes in our youth population. Because of this situation, the American Youth Commission, in its investigation of the needs of young people, has conducted extensive studies of the problems of this particular group. Beginning with careful inquiry into the conditions and needs of Negro youth in the country as a whole, these studies have centered around the question, "How does the fact of being born a Negro affect the developing personality of a boy or girl?"

The project, carried on over a period of three years, has resulted in a number of publications. *In a Minor Key*, by Ira DeA. Reid, presents in compact form much of the general information now available about American Negro youth. It was followed by four volumes on the personality development of Negroes, reporting studies carried on concurrently in different sections of the country and using methods of research especially adapted to the conditions of the various areas. These four volumes are:

Children of Bondage: The Personality Development of Negro Youth in the Urban South, by Allison Davis and John Dollard

Negro Youth at the Crossways: Their Personality Development in the Middle States, by E. Franklin Frazier

Growing Up in the Black Belt: Negro Youth in the Rural South, by Charles S. Johnson

Color and Human Nature: Negro Personality Development in a Northern City, by W. Lloyd Warner, Buford H. Junker, and Walter A. Adams

An additional published report, *Thus Be Their Destiny*, by J. Howell Atwood, Donald W. Wyatt, Vincent J. Davis, and Ira D. Walker, contains brief studies of Negro young people in three communities. Other volumes in the series include *Negro Youth*, a mimeographed bibliography of unpublished theses on the social and economic backgrounds of Negro youth, by Ira DeA. Reid, and *The Atlanta Negro*, a mimeographed collection of data on the Negro population of Atlanta, Georgia, by Joseph A. Pierce, assisted by Marion M. Hamilton.

Eli S. Marks, who served as statistician and member of the research staff of the study of the rural South, has prepared a special monograph entitled, "Rural Negro Youth in Greene County, Georgia," available in manuscript form. E. Franklin Frazier also has unpublished materials regarding the Harlem community in New York City.

The present volume summarizes the chief findings of the entire project and suggests their implications for our national life. The author, Robert L. Sutherland, served as associate director of the Commission in charge of studies of Negro youth, which were begun under the former director of the Commission, Homer P. Rainey, now president of the University of Texas. Dr. Sutherland, formerly professor of sociology at Bucknell University, is now director of the Hogg Foundation's educational lectureship and mental health program administered by the University of Texas.

For assistance in planning and conducting the investigations on which these reports are based, the Commission is indebted to many individuals and organizations. Acknowledgments are due to the authors of the various reports, the other members of the staff, and those individuals and institutions whose assistance is cited by the respective authors. In addition, mention should be made of the services of a special advisory committee which was called together early in 1938 to assist in organizing the project. Will W.

Alexander, vice president of the Julius Rosenwald Fund and consultant on minority groups, Office of Production Management, served as chairman of this committee. The other committee members, in addition to several of the scholars who later joined the staff, were Ambrose Caliver, senior specialist in Negro education, United States Office of Education; George A. Lundberg, of the faculty of Bennington College; Fred McCuistion, southern field agent, General Education Board; Charles Thompson, dean, College of Liberal Arts, Howard University; Robert C. Weaver, chief, Negro Employment and Training Branch, Labor Division, Office of Production Management; and Caroline Zachry, director of research, Progressive Education Association.

To the authors of the several volumes, many of whom are distinguished members of the Negro race, as well as to their research staffs, the American Youth Commission is indebted for work which it believes to have special significance for the welfare of this country. To Dr. Sutherland as director of the project special gratitude is due for his unfailing concern, not only for method and materials of research, but also for the human aspects of the problems with which the studies are concerned.

The American Youth Commission was established in 1935 by the American Council on Education, from which it received a mandate to:

1. consider all the needs of youth and appraise the facilities and resources for serving those needs;

2. plan experiments and programs which will be most helpful in solving the problems of youth;

3. popularize and promote desirable plans of action through publications, conferences, and demonstrations.

As in the case of other staff reports prepared for the Commission, the author of the present volume is responsible for the statements which are made; they are not necessarily endorsed by the Commission or by its Director. The Director does take responsibility for the organization of all research projects, the selection of staff, and the approval of staff reports as meriting publication. The Commission is responsible for the determination of the general areas in which research is conducted under its auspices, and from time to time it adopts and publishes reports which represent specifically the conclusions and recommendations of the Commission.

FLOYD W. REEVES
Director

ACKNOWLEDGMENTS

THE COOPERATION of the entire staff of the American Youth Commission's study of Negro youth is here acknowledged with deepest appreciation. Those who participated in each study are listed in the various volumes. To the advisory committee given on page vii of the Foreword special thanks are given. To President Mordecai Johnson of Howard University, and to Will W. Alexander, consultant on minority groups, Office of Production Management, the author is particularly grateful for reading and criticism of manuscripts.

For assistance at one or many points in the development of the project the author is grateful to Ruth Shonle Cavan, Rockford, Illinois; Horace R. Cayton, Good Shepherd Community Center, Chicago; Wilton P. Chase, Woman's College, University of North Carolina; Helen E. Davis, Commission on Teacher Education, American Council on Education; Philip L. Harriman, Bucknell University; T. Arnold Hill, assistant director of Negro affairs, National Youth Administration; Forrest E. Keller, West Virginia University; T. Ernest Newland, Pennsylvania Department of Education; E. B. Reuter, State University of Iowa; T. J. Woofter, Jr., Federal Security Agency; and to Herbert Blumer, Ernest Burgess, Robert J. Havighurst, and L. L. Thurstone, all of the University of Chicago.

The encouragement, the technical suggestions regarding methods, and the careful reading of manuscripts by the former director of the American Youth Commission, Homer P. Rainey, and his assistant, Arthur L. Brandon, and by their successors, Floyd W. Reeves and Paul T. David, were of inestimable value. M. M. Chambers, D. L. Harley, and Roma K. McNickle, of the American Youth Commission, and Dorothy Leemon and Marjorie P. Putney, of the American Council on Education, have assisted in converting research reports into interesting human documents.

ROBERT L. SUTHERLAND
Associate Director for Studies of Negro Youth

CONTENTS

FOREWORD v
ACKNOWLEDGMENTS ix
WHAT THE NEGRO STUDIES ARE AND ARE NOT xiii

Part I
Things as They Are

   I. COLOR AND NATIONAL SOLIDARITY 3
  II. YOUTH'S WORLD—WHITE AND BLACK 6
 III. THOSE WHO HAVE SHARED THE AMERICAN DREAM 17
 IV. THOSE WHO HAVE BEEN ISOLATED FROM THE AMERICAN DREAM 31
  V. LEARNING HOW TO BE BLACK IN A WHITE WORLD 40
 VI. HIGH VISIBILITY AND STATUS 60
VII. WHAT DOES IT ALL ADD UP TO? 65

Part II
Changes to Be Made

VIII. CHANGING THE STEREOTYPES 79
 IX. CHANGING LOWER-CLASS STANDARDS 96
  X. CHANGING NEGRO EDUCATION, SOCIAL WORK, AND RELIGION 110

NOT BY WAY OF SUMMARY 133

WHAT THE NEGRO STUDIES ARE AND ARE NOT

JOE LOUIS, Aunt Jemima, Rochester, Bigger Thomas, Uncle Tom, Booker T. Washington, James Weldon Johnson, Marian Anderson, Paul Robeson—these names do not belong together and yet each stands for a Negro personality well known in American life. One or more of the people named usually have a close relationship to the ideas of the white person about the Negro. The chances are great that the man in the street forming his notions from hearsay or from very limited observation, will think of Negroes according to the older stereotypes of benign Uncle Tom, happy-go-lucky Jim, or shiftless and delinquent Sam or Mary.

THE NEED FOR INCLUSIVE STUDIES

Probably because sweeping generalizations have been more plentiful than facts, Negro youth have often been misunderstood. They have been misunderstood by the sentimental reformer who sees in them only virtue waiting for the fetters of bad environment to be released. They have been misunderstood also by the moralist who, shocked by their rates of immorality, violence, and crime, considers them representatives of a lower branch of humanity; misunderstood by the enthusiastic educator who, after giving them opportunities for learning, laments the number who drop by the wayside; and even misunderstood by the research specialist whose statistics on housing, health, employment, and dependency are numerically sound but sociologically fragmentary. Still more surprising, they are often misunderstood by the leaders of their own race who, being at the top themselves, misinterpret the life of the lower-class masses.

For years the Negro has been a problem in Sunday school quarterlies, textbooks, and public addresses, but an understanding of the full and exact nature of the problem has seldom been attempted. Typically, these approaches have lumped all twelve million Negroes—black, brown, and light yellow, rich and poor, good and bad—together as a homogeneous group deserving the white man's sympathy, contempt, or assistance. Though much good (and some harm) has been done by these partial views, no statesmanlike approach can be made without a considerably broader scientific understanding.

Attempts have recently been made by various individuals, government agencies, and private foundations to attain and present a more inclusive view of the status of Negro youth. Among them is the American Youth Commission's study, the findings of which are presented in the volumes listed in the Foreword, and in the present summary volume.

THE PROBLEM AND THE MAIN ASSUMPTIONS

"What does it mean to be born a Negro?" This problem and its implications have been the center of the Commission's special studies of Negro youth. Translated into the more formal terms of the research worker, the problem has been stated: "What are the effects, if any, upon the personality development of Negro youth of their minority racial status?"

RACE: BIOLOGICAL OR SOCIOLOGICAL?

The staff tried to avoid the horns of the proverbial dilemma as to whether race is a biological or a social fact. On the one hand, if race is a biological matter, it should be studied with reference to genetic traits and not social definition and attitude. On the other hand, if race is a socially defined affair, it should be studied in terms of attitudes and not chromosomes.

Fortunately, there is room for a middle position between the two horns of this dilemma. The Negro problem is a race problem not in the sense that a purity of Negroid traits has given the American colored person a unique biological nature which makes him behave differently from white people, but rather in that being all or any part Negroid in appearance (the biological fact) has given him a condition of "high visibility" which enables others to identify him and place him in a special position in society (the sociological fact).

To make this position clear the staff assumed that (1) the Negro in America came from one of the biological subspecies of Homo sapiens commonly known as race, but that (2) there was a wide range of physical variation among the African slaves brought to this country, (3) there was still less a pure type when Caucasian, Indian, and Negro blood mixed both legally and extramaritally during the early history of the New World, (4) at the present time many persons called colored have far more white or Indian blood than Negroid while others are closer to the original stock, and (5) the only thing which nearly all Negroes have in common is a biological label of darker pigmentation and different hair texture by which white society can identify and set them apart.

Since, being "set apart" is not a biological but a social matter, the term "race" quickly becomes more of a sociological than a physical concern. "What it *means* to be born a Negro" refers, therefore, primarily to the way communities regard Negro youth and how they regard themselves. The research problem is a question of how differently one acts when from his earliest days he is made to feel different and often inferior because of the attitudes of others toward him.

OTHER ASSUMPTIONS

The staff did not begin its work with the assumption that being a Negro is the most important factor in the personality development of Negro youth. To avoid such a bias most of the area studies were concerned with all of the factors involved in personality, and, indeed in many cases, racial attitudes were found to be of secondary importance.

Nor did the staff begin its work with the assumption that the Negro occupies an entirely unique position in American society. There are other much smaller minority groups whose history is different but whose problems of adjustment are not unlike many of those experienced by Negro youth. Since the investigation had to be limited, no references were made to the other groups even though some of the findings would no doubt fit accurately.

When the staff introduced the term "personality development" in its definition of the research project, it meant by "personality" the whole of one's behavior traits as expressed in social relations.

Or, personality may be defined as the organization of the individual's traits, habits, and attitudes which determine his social role. By social role is meant the social position and function which the person comes to occupy and play as a result of his interaction within the society of which he is a member. Of special interest in this study is the person's conception of himself in so far as this conception reflects and determines his social role. The complete organization of traits of a given personality, that is to say, all of the factors which enter into the social role which he plays, would in a particular case be traced to a complex set of physiological and socio-psychological factors.

Although the focus of attention in the studies was upon Negro youth of the adolescent period, the beginning of traits at an earlier age was studied and their development beyond adolescence followed.

living (not just wealth, but whatever symbols the upper levels hold important) then he, or at least his children or grandchildren, gains admittance to social participation in the high levels. But in a caste relationship social climbing from one caste to another is not permitted. The separation is arbitrary and permanent. Even if a member of the lower caste acquires many of the symbols of the higher living level, he is excluded from participation in higher caste life so long as he possesses the one symbol (usually but not always physical) which has developed in the society as an arbitrary means of separating the two groups.

In Germany and German-controlled Europe a concerted effort is being made to separate Jews from the rest of the population according to this caste principle. The separation is becoming categorical and the movement from one caste to another is prohibited. The only difficulty the Nazis have encountered in their effort to reorganize their society has been the absence of any standard physical trait by which Jews could always be identified and held in their low-caste position.

In the United States, the Negro has been held to a caste position more easily because of his color. Though many European immigrants came to this country with as little knowledge of American life as had Negro slaves, they have within two or three generations become absorbed into the general life of the community and many of them have risen to high position. Individual Negroes have, likewise, become educated, acquired "culture," developed well-organized family life, become well-to-do economically, and acquired all of the other value symbols of the superior caste group, but because they can be marked by their color (and the upper caste has continued to use this as a categorical label) they have been held apart. In short, in a *class system* individuals can move from one level to another by acquiring the proper symbols. In a *caste society* mobility is not permitted

Since the importance of social class and cas[te]
became increasingly apparent as the study
following chapters will be clearer if these te[rms]
at the outset.

CASTE AND CLASS CONCEPTS D[EFINED]

There are almost as many definitions of
"class" and "caste," as there are of the term[s.]
For our purposes a rather simple distinction
a *caste society* persons are born into one gr[oup]
and, by virtue of being so placed and regard[ed]
merit, they have certain rights and privil[eges]
limitations. Members of the higher levels i[n the]
hierarchy of relationships come to think o[f being]
naturally and innately superior to the memb[ers of lower]
levels and, consequently, expect the society t[o treat them]
with superior privileges while members of
are made to perform the less pleasant tasks
lower grade of privileges and rewards for
There is very little mobility from one leve[l to another be-]
cause some external label, like color or nose
(a tattoo mark would do just as well), is us[ed to identify]
and hold in their place those who were bo[rn into a lower]
level.

In a *class system* there is also a social hier[archy and those]
up above feel superior to those down belo[w. The main]
difference between the two systems of stratifi[cation is that]
separation is less rigid and the amount of ind[ividual mobility]
from one level to another is far greater in a c[lass system. The]
greater mobility is made possible by the fact
stigmata, like color, is used as a permanent
bership in a lower or higher level of the s[ociety. One may]
be born into a lower social class and there[fore start with]
social and economic handicaps and limitat[ions, but if he]
gradually acquires the symbols of middle

so long as the individual possesses the symbol which has been used to separate the groups.

In this volume the term "castelike" is used in describing the relations of the Negro and white groups. This has been done because the separation of the two groups is neither complete nor uniform. For example, in not all states is interracial marriage illegal. In not all states are the two races segregated educationally. In some communities Negroes hold high positions in government, in business, in the professions, and in artistic endeavor. But in spite of the fact that the degree of social participation varies for the Negro from place to place and varies to some extent according to individual merit, there is still a constancy about the relationship. Having the label of being a Negro does make a difference anywhere in the United States. There are either formal restrictions or informal subtle limitations placed upon one so identified regardless of what other traits he possesses. In this sense, and in spite of variations, there is ample evidence of the arbitrary operation of the caste principle. To describe this situation, the term "castelike relationship" has been used.

THE AREAS AND THE METHODS

Movement of Negroes northward and cityward has been so pronounced that within a single decade increases of more than 100 per cent occurred in Chicago and New York and nearly 200 per cent in Detroit. These percentages are misleading, however, if other facts are not also kept in mind. In spite of the migration, the rural South is still the home of most Negro youth.

In order to find out how they behave in their traditional home in the South, how they become adjusted to the new world of northern cities, and how they live in the in-between places, the areas chosen for the study included (1) the rural South, (2) three cities in the South, (3) two cities in the middle states, (4) two large cities in the North, and (5) two small cities in the North (few Negroes live in rural communities in the North or in the middle states).

In every area an effort was made to draw cases about equally from boys and girls, from the different educational levels, and from the different social classes.

The methods of studying factors in the personality development of Negro youth included:

    detailed socio-psychiatric case studies

    less detailed sociological life histories involving four to eight interviews with the same person

    briefer social histories secured through the use of the guided interview technique

    life histories drawn from the records of social agencies and psychiatric clinics

    the group interview and participant observer techniques for the purpose of studying group interaction and the role of the person in the group

    questionnaires, both oral and written

    intelligence tests, social attitude tests, color preference rating devices, and similar mass techniques

    ecological and cultural analyses of the community setting with particular attention given to the values involved in the local processes of social stratification.

The directors of the different area studies were free to develop whatever methods they thought appropriate to conditions in their localities. Through frequent staff conferences in Washington, New York, and Chicago, attended by consultants and members of the advisory committee, the staff kept itself informed about the methods employed in the various studies and maintained a common understanding regarding the definition of the problem.

As a result of these conferences the research methods of the different area directors became increasingly similar, and yet each director contributed some distinctive approach or emphasis which has been partly responsible for the fact that the published reports supplement rather than repeat each other.

Allison Davis and John Dollard, working from ethnological and psychoanalytic points of view, studied a few cases intensively and went thoroughly into the question of the relation of personality and social stratification. Their intensive personality studies in cities of the Deep South were made against a background of community material collected in a previous study and now published under the title, *Deep South: A Study of Social Class and Color Caste in a Southern City*.[1]

Charles S. Johnson and his staff used a previous study of more than 1,000 rural counties as a background for the sampling of communities and cases within eight southern counties which represent all of the principal types of southern rural situations in which Negro youth grow to maturity.[2] After sample cases were carefully selected interviews and attitude tests were used to reveal the way personalities develop in this setting.

W. Lloyd Warner and his staff depended upon a recent two-year study conducted in Chicago by Warner, Horace R. Cayton, and a large staff to provide the community material. With this as a background Warner developed a set of criteria by which the life situations of given Negro youth could be roughly characterized. Within each situation he then defined the typical patterns of adjustment commonly found among the cases which his staff examined. Although the number of cases within each situation was

---

[1] By Allison Davis, Burleigh B. Gardner, and Mary R. Gardner (Chicago: University of Chicago Press, 1941).

[2] The areas investigated by the Johnson staff included the following types: (1) active, flourishing plantation area (Coahoma and Bolivar counties, Miss.); (2) decadent plantation area (Greene County, Ga., and Macon County, Ala.); (3) nonplantation, single-crop area (Madison County, Ala.); (4) urban type cotton area (Shelby County, Tenn.); and (5) diversified farming area (Johnston County, N.C., and Davidson County, Tenn.).

not large enough for absolute accuracy in describing adjustment patterns, yet this scheme of analysis with its emphasis upon objective criteria and personality adjustment in terms of observable culture patterns has contributed an approach of great interest which could well be tested in a still more extensive study.

E. Franklin Frazier, using thirteen volumes of unpublished material which he assembled for Mayor La Guardia's Commission on Conditions in Harlem in 1935 following the race riots in Harlem, proceeded from this background to examine New York as a center of social unrest and social movements among Negro youth. Dr. Frazier has not yet carried out his plan of publishing a special volume on social movements in Harlem, but has used some of this material as a basis of comparison in his report on the cities of the middle states. In his published study Dr. Frazier and his staff gave special attention to the way in which group interaction reveals the social role of the person. He reported the processes of personality development in terms of the principal social relationships of youth in the community.

In Greensboro, North Carolina, the research staff examined intensively the social strivings of a mobile, middle-class group of youth. In Galesburg, Illinois, and in Milton, Pennsylvania, the investigators tried to find out how small northern communities with a strong liberal tradition were influencing the personality development of Negro youth.

The published reports go into the question of methodology within each area and in certain cases a still more complete statement of method is available in mimeographed form at the office of the American Council on Education.

PURPOSE OF THIS BOOK

Since the methods of study in the different areas were not identical this summary volume cannot give precise generalizations supported by columns of figures. Rather, its purpose is to interpret for the reader the various observations, insights, and hypotheses which the different reports have contributed to the central problem. Giving the "picture as a whole" this summary will emphasize the new ways of looking at race relations which these studies have revealed. A new concept, a new method of analysis, a new basis for judgment may prove to be as valuable as statistical facts. Some day personality traits may be counted and the processes involved in acquiring a prejudice or a frustration measured (Charles Johnson's attitude tests made a contribution in this direction), but, in general, the studies in this series reveal processes more in the case study than in the survey fashion. The observations to be reported in the following chapters will therefore be based largely upon insights revealed to our trained investigators through an intimate acquaintance with different Negro youth growing up under different circumstances.

IMPLEMENTATION

In a way which may displease some social scientists this report will deal with methods of control and improvement. Especially in the second half of the book, general recommendations will be made, specific projects suggested, and advice given to agencies at work in the field. This is in keeping with the policy of the American Youth Commission which is to formulate a program of action on the basis of new insights gained through research.

CRITICS IN ADVANCE

In order to benefit from the criticism of the advisory committee, the original consultants, and others especially capable of passing judgment, this manuscript was sent to thirty critics in mimeographed form. As a result of their suggestions many changes have been made. In several instances the critic has been quoted directly so that the reader may have the advantage of different points of view as he goes along.

PART I

THINGS AS THEY ARE

CHAPTER I

COLOR AND NATIONAL SOLIDARITY

GOVERNMENTS generally recognize that when the external security of a nation is in danger, the importance of maintaining internal unity is greatly increased; they adopt different methods, however, of achieving this objective. Required conformity is common in totalitarian states; in a democracy coercion, though not entirely absent, is emphasized less than voluntary loyalty.

In our democracy all persons are expected to accept civic responsibility and are presumed to have an equal opportunity to rise to positions of importance in national life. Equal opportunity, personal liberty, and a society that is classless, casteless, and without barrier to individual success through personal merit—these are glittering terms in a democracy, spoken freely from the platform and over the microphone.

But for a tenth of the population in this country these terms cannot be taken too literally. When democratic rights, privileges, responsibilities, and rewards mean one thing to people of light pigmentation and another to those of darker hue, the seemingly superficial matter of skin color becomes involved in any consideration of national unity and security.

A one-tenth minority is a sizeable one, with which even a totalitarian state would reckon. A democratic state, depending more upon free cooperation, must give special attention to its minorities in times both of peace and of conflict. Hence, this book assumes that the Negro is of national importance and interest to America, that the way he thinks and acts, the way his social attitudes and personal outlook have developed, should be known—especially at a time when all parts of the nation must work together.

And what will happen after the crisis—this, too, is a pertinent question. A nation intent upon an immediate goal tends to forget about what lies ahead. The well-being of all youth should be protected by long-time planning, but Negro youth have a special stake in the future. When jobs shrank in numbers and pay envelopes in size following the first World War, many Negro youth were asked to step out of their traditional types of employment as waiters, bellboys, and laborers, while white unemployed took their places. Negro leaders would not have regretted this change if, at the same time, they had been given corresponding freedom to compete as individuals for whatever types of work were open, but caste restrictions though relaxed at the bottom were not relaxed at the top. Negro youth had been deprived of many lower-caste jobs without being admitted to higher-caste opportunities.

During a crisis when changes occur rapidly and manpower is needed, opportunities for Negro youth will be increased to some extent. Will these gains be undermined following the crisis, and new forms of restrictions invented as after the last war? Will the very patterns of totalitarian coercion in Europe which our nation is challenging find their way into our own attitudes toward minority groups? The present is none too early to consider these possible consequences and prepare measures of control.

How do America's twelve million Negroes react to these matters? Do they think they belong to the common life of the nation? Do they feel that they are a part of its defense effort and will be rewarded for their loyalty with increased freedom to live as other Americans do? Or, do they still interpret their role in American society as a special one?

And, what does the white group think about this minority of twelve million? Do they still regard them as such a happy-go-lucky lot, so simple in their thought processes that they can be safely relied upon in time of peace and effectively controlled in time of crisis?

If Negro youth are beginning to sense not only their present insecurity but that of the future, are they becoming ready listeners to rightists, leftists, fifth-columnists, and others who promise Utopia through radical change? What effects are education, social welfare work, and the policies of government having upon their attitude? In the following pages Negro youth will speak for their group in answer to these and other questions.

This volume is not a survey of population, wages, or number of rooms to a family; it is rather a study of the outlook of Negro youth on racial matters and other important concerns in their lives. We shall begin with the cultural setting of Negro youth—part of which they share with white youth and part of which is their special heritage.

CHAPTER II

YOUTH'S WORLD—
WHITE AND BLACK

STUDIES IN personality adjustment have often stressed childhood training, family relations, and inherited traits, but seldom have they shown the relationship between the dreams youth inherit from a culture of optimism and the frustrations they encounter in matching their dreams with reality. The statements below, typical of white youth who are in doubt about their future, seem strangely inconsistent with the traditional concept of opportunity in a land of plenty. This inconsistency is a key to understanding many traits and problems in personality development. Is such inconsistency common for both white and colored youth?

WHITE YOUTH AND THE AMERICAN DREAM

As a background and basis for comparison, certain broad aspects of the culture which affect the development of white youth will be described before attention is given to the world of Negro young people.

> This job I have is a dead-end proposition and I'm getting tired of it.
>
> . . .
>
> I have finished college and have a white-collar "position," but the skilled laborer in the plant is getting higher pay than I do.
>
> . . .
>
> Government projects may be all right as a temporary substitute for real work, but I am anxious to get started in a line of my own.
>
> . . .

I seem to be the lucky one. My promotions have been as regular as my Dad's were, but of course Dad's position may have had something to do with the breaks I got.

The "American dream," a symbol of society's definition of what is good and expected in American life, bears heavily upon the individual youth as a compulsion to "succeed." From the Horatio Alger success stories to their modern counterpart in Major Bowes' weekly discovery of hidden talent, Dale Carnegie's formula for economic and social climbing, and Orphan Annie's rewards for virtuous living, American youth have been imbued with the notion of personal achievement.

A student of culture could make a long list of influences which have supported this idea in the minds of millions of young people. Moving pictures quite generally present in their setting or in their concluding scene a suggestion of success and happiness—a higher standard of living than the majority of their audiences enjoy or the heroine experienced at the opening of the play. Many magazines and radio programs feature success stories. Public speakers, ministers, YMCA leaders, Boy Scout masters, service club speakers, all appeal to the idea that personal merit will be rewarded with advancement and honor. The history of our nation and its prominent personalities strengthen the reader's expectancy of victory over hardship. The westward movement with the pioneer's conquering of great barriers, the rise of cities, and the coming of captains of industry, financial tycoons, and political giants whose boyhood was spent in overalls have strengthened youth's desire for and assurance of success.

Greatest of these influences has perhaps been the schools themselves. Their program has been based upon the objective of personal improvement. It has always been taken for granted that reward will come to him who works hard and merits promotion—promotion from grade to grade in school, and, in life after school, from one rung of the economic and social ladder to the next. Commencement speakers have called upon youth to shoulder the burdens of the nation and in so doing have implied that they were thinking of the graduates not as obscure filling-station attendants but as business and civic leaders. Many textbooks are loaded with heroes but have little or no concern for the common man. Furthermore, the prejudice of the schools and of our culture generally has been in favor of white-collar jobs. It is not an accident that the stenographer has looked down upon the factory girl, although the latter may have a pay check twice as large.

Even in exclusive social circles, high position has been attained in part through personal effort. Although family background is of importance, birth counts for less in the United States than in many other countries, and individual attainments, economic and otherwise, count for more. If our society has not developed as entirely classless, it has at least been considered as an open class system in which movement from one level to another is free to the deserving. If upper-class circles have held their requirements for admission high and have prolonged the probationary period for social climbers, the middle classes at least have welcomed all who attain family respectability and economic success.

Much modern advertising in the United States has been grounded upon the individual's desire to rise socially and the expectancy that he will do so if he acquires the right symbols of success. From this point of view, the appearance and model of his car are as important as its internal efficiency, and his address in the right residential district has social value. In some communities his membership in certain churches and clubs carries greater prestige than membership in others. He must also act like a person with "culture." All of these facts are common knowledge and, although they are not always discussed, they influence a person's organization of his daily life as well as his more distant objectives.

The tremendous power of these pressures upon American youth in the past will never be accurately measured, but no one doubts that the desire of youth to live in better houses than their parents owned, have better jobs than their fathers held, and achieve ever higher social positions has been an important incentive relied upon by the school, the church, and the family to stimulate ambitious endeavor and moral conformity.

All worked smoothly in this national scheme as long as reality kept pace with the dream. For years every community contained so many living illustrations of achievement made possible by education, hard work, and a life of respectability that the high school assembly speaker had little trouble in proving his point. Even an occasional failure was not too serious because the prevailing culture gave the individual ample opportunity for second trials and rewarded his ultimate success with still greater honor. "Life begins at forty" was good news for those who had met with earlier adversity.

Just as the dream of world peace was shattered by the wars of 1914 and 1939, so the old faith in individual success was followed by disillusionment during the period of widespread unemployment beginning in 1929. Indices to personal disorganization such as suicide, delinquency, and migrancy showed an increase, perhaps not so great as might have been expected because prompt action by the government provided a measure of social security as a substitute for individual achievement.

Personal disillusionment may have been greatly accentuated by the depression of 1929, but even this financial debacle was not responsible for its origin. Already during the two-car-garage era of the twenties the tightening of class lines was clearly apparent. Studies of that decade pictured

America as a land with rich opportunity for limited numbers and with millions of low-paying jobs for the masses. Boys might still dream of becoming bank presidents and prepare themselves for the title, but the positions were well filled and the waiting list was long. During the twenties, when production and financial prosperity were greatest for the nation as a whole, there were at times several million unemployed, of whom youth formed a high proportion.

In the Maryland youth survey made for the American Youth Commission, the evidence of social stratification as opposed to advancement through individual merit was convincing. The sons and daughters of farm hands and unskilled laborers proved to have a very slight chance for higher education or well-paid positions in comparison with the children of the smaller group of professional and business leaders. Yet, in spite of the fact that the odds are weighted many times against them, girls and boys of both country and city continue to indulge in the typical American dream of white collars, automobiles, and homes of their own. This fact was presented strikingly in the diagram of the Maryland report, *Youth Tell Their Story,* which pictured the gap that separates the "jobs youth want" from the "jobs youth get."

This discrepancy between the encouragement our culture gives individuals to hitch their kite strings to a star and the reality of what they actually attain may have a much closer relationship to the prevalence of inferiority complexes, personal frustration, compensatory behavior, and even antisocial conduct than has been generally recognized.

In the 1940 presidential election there was evidence that the political parties were awakening to some of these problems and becoming aware of the tightening of class lines. The educational and community agencies have made an attempt to cope with the conditions which are modifying America's traditional dream of individual initiative and social reward. But in the classroom the child is still generally taught how to succeed, not how to absorb failures and find substitute satisfactions. He is tutored in techniques for better individual competition more than in the arts of group cooperation. The physical setup of the classroom, the grading system, the rapid increase in many types of interscholastic competition, and the awards at commencement are out of gear with a culture which is now changing rapidly. Business, government, and community organization are operating more and more on a corporate basis; education is still largely an individualistic affair, although many schools and teachers are now trying to give their pupils a new type of incentive, outlook, and educational experience.

The present world of white youth must be redefined if the experiences through which young people are moving are to be understood. The effects of economic change upon the church, the factory, and the family have been thoroughly traced, but little attention has been given to such effects upon the personalities of boys and girls who have shared in the American dream but have been debarred from its achievement.

The coming of the war boom in business activity with many jobs and high wages for high school graduates has again changed the world of youth. The changes which have come, instead of solving youth's problems, involve new forces as blind to the welfare of the individual as were the forces of the depression. Some youth whose older brothers were frustrated because they did not succeed in attaining the American standard are now finding themselves blessed almost overnight with a chance for big pay and a car of their own.

Jack S. of Redmond, Washington, could find no job during the summer vacation of 1940, worked for a few weeks as a berry picker at a dollar or less a day, dreamed of becoming a doctor but could figure out no way of realizing his dream, and finally accepted a commonplace routine. After his high school graduation in 1941 his fortune had changed. Induced to take a short course in riveting at a vocational high school, he found his services in demand at the Boeing Aircraft plant in Seattle where, after a short time, he makes eight to ten dollars a day with overtime figured in. Unprepared for a standard of income he had not expected to reach for at least fifteen years, he is spending most of his earnings on a car, a girl, and a good time. The admonitions of his older brother and father who repeatedly tell him of their hard-time experiences have had little effect. Sudden prosperity is teaching Jack S. very little about life, and is in no way preparing him for the loss of his job if peace or panic replace war activity.

Not all youth are having even this breathing spell of prosperity. Many not living in defense centers are still working long hours in chain stores wondering when they can marry the district manager's daughter or experience some other economic miracle. Furthermore, those youth inducted into military service must of necessity postpone still longer their dreams of comfortable family life, of economic success, and of community leadership.

In spite of great improvements in the way the nation is meeting the present war crisis as compared with the last, forces blind to the welfare of the individual seem still to be too much in control. If frustrated personalities emerge into Hitlers and Mussolinis in national affairs, and into their smaller counterparts in every community, then preparedness should be defined as much in terms of personality traits as military tactics.

Only as individuals are rewarded in their early development of self-control, long-time planning, high standards of character, ability to sacrifice now for later gain, and ability to work toward group goals can we expect to produce stable persons as followers and leaders. And, if society wants these traits in persons it must maintain community conditions which will permit such development. Sudden shifts from widespread unemployment to an artificial and possibly temporary prosperity will not help. And continuing to revere most highly the personal attainment of wealth when loyalty to group objectives is needed also makes for social loss and frustrated personalities. Communities in particular and the nation in general must decide what they desire to value most and then reward youth who meet this pattern if they want the society and the personalities within it to be in harmony.

If developing a more consistent set of values and cultural influences is an imperative when the welfare of white youth is considered, it becomes a double imperative for the one-tenth of our youth population who are Negro. Far more than is true of white youth, Negro boys and girls have been taught one thing and permitted to do another, they have been accepted verbally and rejected personally, they have been admonished to strive only to find the rewards taken away. These and other traits in our culture which influence the type of persons Negro boys and girls become is from now on our special field of study. How can a democracy be consistent in permitting its youth, both white and colored, to become the type of persons its avowed ideals indicate they should?

NEGRO YOUTH AND THE AMERICAN DREAM

If the cultural approach to an understanding of personality has given insight about the motives and frustrations of white youth, this approach should give still more insight regarding our social orphans of darker hue who are born into but are partially rejected from the "American way." Let some of these youth speak for themselves:

> Fancy clothes, a big car, and a painted house—these things seem to be for white folks, not colored.

· · · ·

> The Army calls for volunteers and its posters tell about the chances to learn a trade, travel, and get promoted, but when we try to get in there is always something the matter with us, or if we do get in, we don't get anywhere.
>
> . . . .
>
> Books on occupations describe all kinds of jobs, but a Negro boy has to cross out many of them from the start.
>
> . . . .
>
> Concerts, lectures, and museums are supposed to teach a better way of living, but they don't do colored kids any good if they can't get in.

These comments are similar to hundreds of statements made by Negro youth who were interviewed in the field studies of this research. Not all Negro youth feel exactly the same way, not all have deliberated on these matters, but protests of one type or another were common in all communities studied.

The stereotyped notion of success which in the past functioned so effectively in motivating white youth to strive for high achievement was not so effective when four million of their number were unemployed. The force of these symbols is weakened still more when it reaches Negro youth, who in most matters and in most places are held at a still greater distance from the good things of life as defined by the prevailing culture.

After reading the four area research studies, Dorothy Canfield Fisher wrote the Introduction to *Native Son* in which she made this comment on the Negro youth problem:

> . . . our American society creates around all youth (as every society does) a continual pressure of suggestion to try to live up to the accepted ideals of the country—such ordinary, traditional, taken-for-granted American ideals as to fight injustice fearlessly; to cringe to no man; to choose one's own life work; to resist with stouthearted self-respect affronts to decent human dignity, whether one's own or others'; to drive ahead toward honestly earned success, all sails spread to the old American wind blowing from the Declaration of Independence. But our society puts Negro youth in the situation of the animal

in the psychological laboratory in which a neurosis is to be caused, by making it impossible for him to try to live up to those never-to-be questioned national ideals, as other young Americans do.[1]

For most young people incentives to achievement are effective only when they are near at hand. One must see a measure of success within reach before he will exert great effort for more. Distant goals may draw the exceptional persons, but most individuals are confirmed in "right" behavior by immediate approval or by what the educator calls obtainable goals.

What rewards are available to Negro youth that will confirm the character traits which a middle-class white society has decided they should have? At least three complicating factors have to some extent isolated them from the common stream of cultural influence.

First, many young Negroes have never experienced the American dream. They have never known a society composed of respectable, law-abiding, industrious, self-reliant families whose ambition has been rewarded by good houses, electric refrigerators, and an improved social status. If youth respond to incentives near at hand, there is little wonder, then, that the behavior of many Negro boys and girls has been controlled by a set of standards foreign and incomprehensible to their white critics.

Second, there are many Negro youth less isolated than those just mentioned. They have had intimations of a "better way of living," through the movies, magazines, radio programs, and schools, but they are profoundly confused, nevertheless, because this way of living seems to bear no relation to their own. The moral which the teacher draws from the history lesson, the poem, or the biography is a moral for white youth, not colored. Frustration therefore

---

[1] Richard Wright, *Native Son* (New York: Harper and Brothers, 1940), "Introduction," p. x.

often results when the goal and the reward are held before Negro youth but a color line which they dare not cross bars them from competing in the struggle.²

Third, even to the extent that the American dream is theoretically accessible to Negro youth, its attainment is made more difficult by unemployment, poor training, and inadequate resources. Though shared by white youth, these handicaps prevail in the experience of the Negro to a disproportionate degree. *In a Minor Key* shows in each succeeding chapter the added handicaps which Negro youth face in their response to the call for self-improvement and well-conducted family life.

The world of youth—white and black—is inconsistent. The critic of another's behavior would do well to inquire into the local culture for an understanding of the intimate pressures to which developing personalities must respond. These cultural pressures and their corresponding rewards of social approval vary in time—it makes a difference whether one grows up in times of depression or prosperity; they vary in place—coming of age in New York is vastly different from adolescence in a rural village; and they vary in the experience of different groups—belonging to "Little Italy," the "Gold Coast," or "Harlem" affects one's outlook in diverse ways. There is little wonder that these varying conditions affect personality. But thus far the analysis of the processes at work has only been generalized. A closer view will bring further insight into what it means under varying circumstances to be born a Negro.

² These statements are not intended to imply that education should adjust Negro youth to accept the barriers of the *status quo*. Rather, education should prepare them to cope with the barriers, find ways around them, and even master techniques for removing them. But to ignore the present reality of the barriers brings frustration and attitudes of futility.

CHAPTER III

THOSE WHO HAVE SHARED THE AMERICAN DREAM

In spite of apparent contradiction, one must acknowledge upon closer analysis that not all Negro youth are in as unhappy circumstances as the preceding generalizations might indicate. Not every Negro youth is complaining about economic matters, or is conscious of a "race problem."

John X., for example, is relatively well-to-do. His father is a college professor, his mother a social worker. In their home are electric lights, plumbing, and modern furniture, and in the attached, heated garage, a new Buick sedan. John has congenial friends and well-trained school teachers, and on Sunday goes to a sedate house of worship.

In time, he will be graduated from high school, then college, then professional school. He will become a doctor, a teacher, a lawyer, or possibly a businessman. His grammar will be correct, his manner polite, his dress in good taste. He will learn how to play contract bridge, be at ease at a tea, and give orders to servants. He will marry well, observe marital ethics (in spite of a certain amount of sophisticated talk), give presents at Christmas time, take a vacation in the summer, and rear his children to become self-respecting members of polite society.

Many aspects of his biography will resemble those of white youth born into upper-middle-class families. True, he will always be a Negro—unless his skin is white and he wishes to "pass"—but, in his daily round of life, caste limitations placed upon his race will concern him less than keeping in the good graces of his own circle of friends or, more probably, in the good graces of the circle just above his in social and economic standing.

This illustration should show that being born a Negro must apparently be thought of in terms of the social and economic positions which the given individual occupies. John X. refutes many of the stereotyped notions about the Negro's lack of efficiency, refinement, stable family life, and ambition. In all of the area studies made by the American Youth Commission, there were a number of John X.'s—enough, in fact, to be considered a small upper-middle- or upper-class group.

For example, there is the Neal family in Natchez, whose income is $250 a month; they own a ten-room house in a neighborhood where the heads of the families are all physicians, dentists, teachers, or businessmen. Mrs. Neal, who has been more zealous than her husband in maintaining family position, is merely putting into practice the class training of her own childhood. She was born into a farm-owning, upper-middle-class family in Mississippi. After completing the graded school in a nearby town, she was sent to Natchez to high school and then to a Negro college in Jackson, Mississippi. All of her brothers—she had no sisters—are interior decorators in Cleveland.

Like all middle-class Negroes in the Deep South, Mrs. Neal is quick to distinguish her family from lower-class people by pointing out that none of her brothers has ever been "in jail." She makes several other important class claims. Her father and mother are very light people with straight hair. They were among the six "oldest and most influential" Negro families in the county. They had a relatively high income; when Mrs. Neal returned from college and was offered a position in the local school, her mother would not allow her to work for the small salary paid a Negro teacher. Even more indicative of her class position is the fact that her mother gave her a "very strict" rearing; she was allowed to associate with only one girl in the county, who was from the "best" family, and she was never permitted to go to a dance or a frolic.

Similar cases could be cited from each community investigated. E. Franklin Frazier found in Washington, D.C., that approximately 6 per cent of the families enjoyed a type of employment appropriate to upper-middle- or upper-class standards of living, although actual acceptance into the exclusive circles was determined by a number of factors in addition to occupation. In the eight rural counties of the South which Charles S. Johnson studied, he found data which disproved the old notion that all rural Negroes belong to the same social level. Although the range of social position is more restricted than in urban communities, there was ample evidence of loosely defined lower-, middle-, and upper-class strata. Those of higher position took more pride than did the others in superior homes, advanced education for their children, better organized family life, and supervised recreation.

These youth and their families are behaving in a manner that would meet the criteria of any white critic of colored behavior. They have shared the American dream and have succeeded in the climb upward. They have self-respect, family pride, ambitions for their children—in fact, everything which education, economic success, and the acquisition of "culture" are supposed to bring. The similarity between their way of life and that of upper-middle-class white youth is so close that no one need ever doubt that Negro youth are capable of responding in the same way as do white youth when surrounded by similar incentives, opportunities, and rewards.

This discovery may come as a surprise to those who have always thought of Negro youth as lax in morals, untrustworthy in employment, and uncouth in personal appearance. They find it hard to conceive of colored youth dressed in expensive but not gaudy clothes, living in homes tastefully decorated, and discussing intelligently new pictures, operas, plays, books, and world affairs. Such behavior simply does not fit the traditional notion, and after a convenient definition of a group becomes fixed in tradition the stereotype often acquires more force than do firsthand observations.

FACTORS LIMITING UPWARD STRIVING

Although the studies of the American Youth Commission have shown that every Negro community is to some extent stratified—that there are middle- and upper-class patterns of conduct as well as the more commonly recognized lower-class living—they have also presented the reasons why the thrust upward has affected so few individuals and why the pull downward has kept such a high proportion of Negro youth in their traditional place. The basic reasons may be summarized under the two headings which follow.

ECONOMIC INSECURITY

The first and cruder factor is not unknown to anyone who observes the conditions of life of Negro youth. What the community recognizes as middle- or upper-middle-class patterns of living are generally possible only when there is a substantial economic base which will provide the members of the family with some leisure, a good education, and adequate housing. And this is something which is not available to high proportions of Negro youth in any community.

Middle-class white families who employ Negro domestics often naïvely hope, and even expect, that their servants will have a personal standard of health, dress, diction, and trustworthiness which will enable them to fit into and support their own standards, particularly in the care of the children. How such behavior can be expected with a six-dollar-a-week wage as the only incentive is a question seldom raised. Notwithstanding their low reward, many colored domestics and other workers do maintain a relatively high standard of efficiency and personal conduct.

In general, however, these studies have revealed repeatedly that the maintenance in Negro community life of standards of living and health in keeping with the "American pattern" requires an income which only a small fraction of Negroes enjoy. The reports have underscored the fact that Negro youth generally start out in life surrounded by physical and social conditions conducive to the kind of behavior which in the past has made them the objects of criticism. Thus the cycle of adverse influences and undesirable social behavior repeats itself generation after generation.

LACK OF SOCIAL PARTICIPATION

Such an emphasis on low economic status as a limiting factor has been made in many books. A second point, however, has often been overlooked; removing the economic disadvantage faced by Negro youth would not in itself solve their problems of personality and group adjustment. Roadhouses, gambling establishments, the highways after midnight, and other places of reckless conduct are not frequented exclusively, nor principally, by the unemployed or by youth on relief. Young people who have money but little or no social training are recognized by any community, white or colored, as constituting a serious aspect of its total youth problem.

Social training is more than a matter of instruction in the teachings of Emily Post. It is a reflection of one's whole complex of living—of his close associates, of the things his neighborhood values highly, and of the way he gets his personal satisfaction and recognition. There is, in other words, no necessary correlation in individual cases between the crude fact of income and class behavior, although *in general* the cycle of bad influences and bad conduct stands unchallenged. However, general averages are not sufficient for a clear understanding of personality processes; it is necessary to see the forces at work in individual cases—social training, intimate influences of clique associates, and emotional experiences during childhood.[1]

Hence it is important to consider the second, more subtle factor that limits upward striving by Negro youth; it is largely a matter of social participation. As Davis and Dollard in *Children of Bondage* explained in such detail and as the other studies confirmed, the child from his earliest experiences is most responsive to the rewards and punishments in the immediate environment of his family and clique relationships. Behavior patterns which bring rewards in the form of physical satisfactions and social approval are early adopted by the child, and there is no inherent tendency within the individual to strive for what a hypothetical "society in general" might call "higher standards."

Ambition is not an automatic yearning for improvement; it is a social product. Youth who are responsive to the middle-class requirements for ambitious striving in their occupation, for conventional morality in family relations, and for the other sorts of behavior commonly attributed to middle-class culture, follow these patterns only if their first efforts to do so have brought approval, and if contrary conduct has brought disapproval or punishment.[2] The Negro youth who has acquired what the established community

---

[1] Although in the area studies attention was given to the physical factors in personality development, and in the southern urban study great stress was laid upon early processes, this concluding volume, which cannot go into all phases of the question thoroughly, must give greater space to those social factors that were found to be especially important. This is not done in disregard of other approaches.

[2] Wilton P. Chase suggests that for the benefit of those interested in the theory of learning, we might go further and say, "Industriousness, initiative, responsibility, aggressiveness, emotionality, and all personality traits are by-products of immediate incentives and interests. Our biggest educational mistake is to assume that they are educable characteristics *per se*."

considers the "better ways of living" has done so because he has been permitted to share or participate in the rewards for such conduct.

FACTORS STIMULATING UPWARD STRIVING

Generally speaking, Negro youth whose lives conform to the "better ways of living" have been born into the upper-middle or upper class or have been influenced by the driving force of someone else's determination that they shall rise in the social scale.

ECONOMIC AND SOCIAL SECURITY

Some Negro youth have been so completely surrounded by middle-class patterns that their expectation of achieving advanced degrees, high professional standing, and an income which will enable them to live as well as, or better than, their parents is taken for granted. As was true in the case of John X., class or caste barriers have not seemed seriously to prevent them from sharing the "American way." Its able proponents have been the family, the school, the church, and most effective of all, the attitudes of neighborhood playmates. In all social contacts competing patterns were excluded, and this manner of living given the right of way. Under such circumstances, a Negro youth fits into the prevailing modes of conduct as naturally as an Eskimo child develops a personality which reflects and perpetuates the culture of his group.

A Negro girl from Alabama, the daughter of a well-to-do physician, told one of the investigators that she had been almost unaware of the seriousness of the race problem until she studied about it in a sociology class at Fisk University. Her parents had given her every cultural advantage in her own home life and her associations had been largely limited to other people similarly situated. She had attended a public school for several years and then a private school, but in neither case did she seem concerned by the fact that they were all-Negro institutions. Her parents had protected her from unpleasant Jim-Crow experiences through traveling only by automobile and arranging in advance for pleasant accommodations with friends in other cities. This girl's dress, her manner of speaking, her poise in social relations, her "cultural" interests, and her ideals for her own family life and the rearing of her children were a natural and expected reflection of a way of life which had been consistently held before her. Seldom are the influences which surround a developing personality as homogeneous as appeared to be true in this case, but there are more than a few young Negroes in any community who have to a large degree had a similar experience.

A CHANCE TO PARTICIPATE

In addition to this "pure" type of case there is a second and more common situation which may yield similar results. It is one in which the influences are mixed, but the more socially acceptable patterns win out. Because of the small size of the middle class in any Negro community and because of the boundaries created by racial segregation, it is often difficult for middle- and upper-class parents to keep their children from taking over some of the ways of lower-class children with whom they associate. In the face of this situation with its mixture of influences, many Negro parents have developed remarkable skill and finesse in selecting the patterns which will be allowed to influence the lives of their children. By appealing to family pride and ideas of class superiority as well as by an outright manipulation of the child's social environment so that he will avoid distracting patterns of conduct as much as possible, they often accomplish such wonders as to make the task of the white parent seem simple.

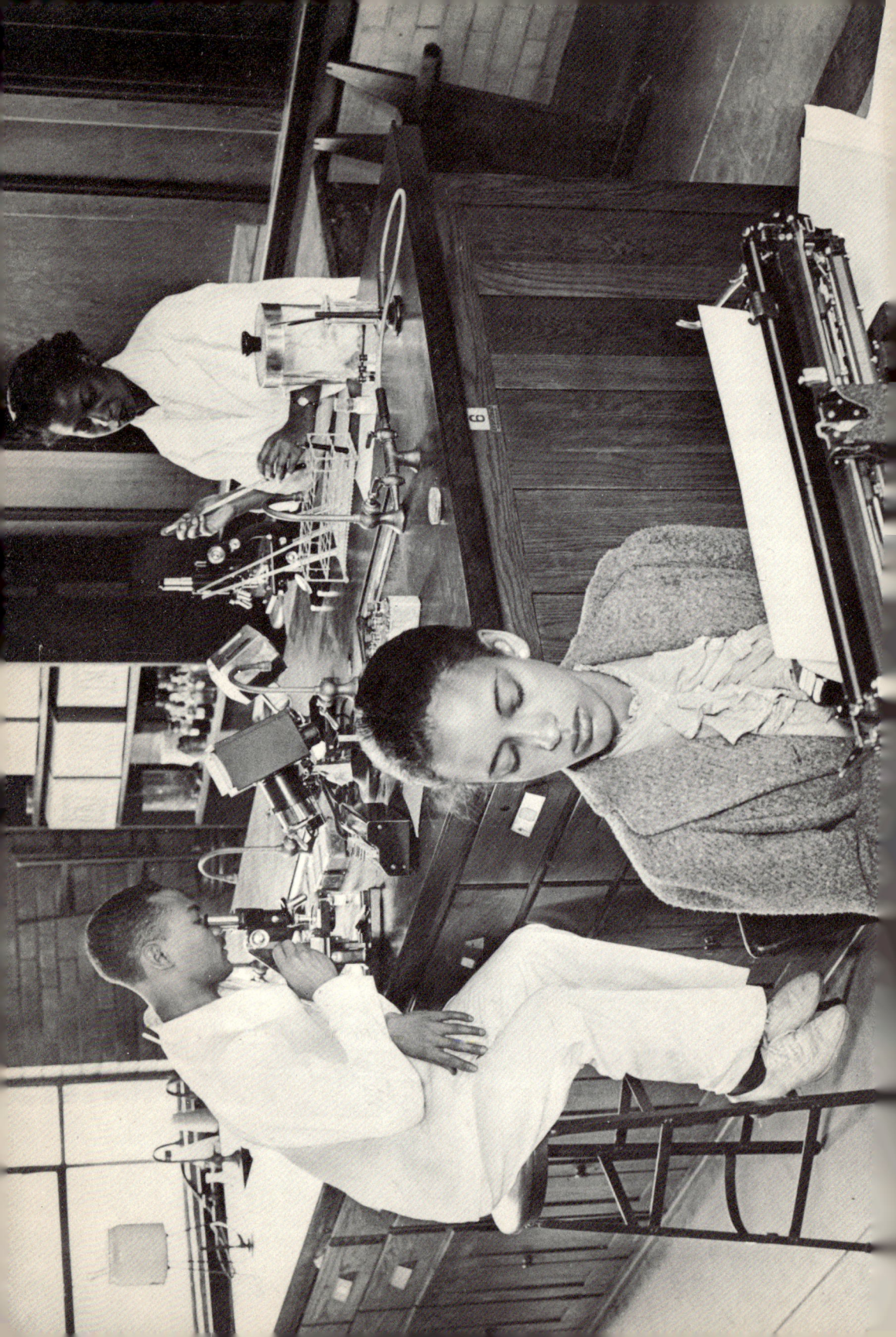

A Mother Forces Her Son to Climb

The success of Chester in attaining upper-middle-class status in New Orleans when he started out in life as a ditch-digger's son is a tribute to the skill of his mother in selecting the environment from which she wished her son to seek approval. Taking advantage of the fact that her son's handicap in size placed him at a disadvantage with the fighting gangs of the lower class, she quickly substituted rewards more in keeping with her determination that he succeed socially. Observers describe Chester's social striving in these terms:

> He flees from lower status and insecurity; once arrived at upper-class participation, he modifies his behavior, using his skills and talents to gain admission, then modeling himself on the boys and girls who are his new associates.

The mother was so successful in directing her son's aggressive tendencies away from gang fighting toward success in school, honors in organized athletics, and participation in the circles of the socially elite that the son soon outdistanced her. In order to protect his new standing, Chester could not bring his school friends home or allow his parents to be invited to their homes. The mother was so proud of her son's attainment that she willingly suffered this gradual loss of intimate association with him and with his friends.

Teachers Help a Gifted Boy

For some Negro youth, participation in a middle-class culture has been more indirect and fortuitous than Chester's. One of the outstanding Negro educators of the present day has a life history which closely parallels the Horatio Alger or the farm-boy-to-president pattern. Born on a one-mule-two-bale cotton farm in South Carolina, he was graduated from the county high school with honors, was awarded a Phi Beta Kappa key during his junior year at a high-ranking eastern college, completed his doctor's degree at an outstanding university, and has subsequently held one prominent position after another.

His climb from lowly economic and social circumstances to well-entrenched membership in upper-class circles cannot be explained on the basis of superior ability alone, for there are many Negro youth of far better than average intellect who, as the social judgments go, "never amount to anything." Nor can his rise be explained on the basis of unusual parental protection and encouragement. Although his parents were "respectable" people in the neighborhood and encouraged their son in his school work, they had no knowledge of higher education nor appreciation of its possible value as a means for his advancement.

In this case the persons who made such ideas effective were his teachers. After having made straight A's in his high school course (at the expense of losing status with his lower-class friends), the boy inquired of a teacher one day, "You have encouraged me in my school work and made me think that I am better than other children, but this is an all-colored school, and how do I really know that I am as good as white students?" The teacher challenged him to answer his own question by competing with white students in a first-ranking college of New England and promised to assist him to make the start financially.

The boy was already a marginal personality in that he had abandoned the interests and satisfactions of his former neighborhood associates and had responded to the approval of his teachers, who represented a different cultural standard. At this point in his development he either had to regain the friendship of his old associates by reverting to their ways of conduct or move ahead in response to the flattering challenge of the teacher.

Once the decision was made to move on, each new school success brought immediate approval both from his new white associates, who were surprised to find such talent in a Negro, and from his newly acquired upper-class Negro friends. It would be as unnatural now for him to revert to lower-class interests as it would be for one of his old cronies suddenly to decide to be a bank president. But when he was first losing status with his carefree, ambitionless, and better accommodated associates in the neighborhood and was experiencing the doubtful substitute satisfaction of his teachers' approval, he was a ready candidate for pressures in either direction. At such a time the influence of a teacher, a social worker, or any other representative of middle-class living had a chance to count for more than the long-time influences of his old associates.

OTHER FACTORS IN ADJUSTMENT

Up to this point in the analysis of why some Negro youth have responded like many white youth to the American dream, two basic factors have been seen in operation. The economic factor is important because only a few colored youth have sufficient means to live according to upper-middle- or upper-class standards. The factor of social participation is likewise important because the individual must have a chance to participate in a culture if he is to follow its standards.

But, are there not other factors? Can personality development be analyzed without reference to variations in innate ability and to variations in childhood experiences of various types? Even in a summary which stresses the social class and social caste approaches passing attention must be given to these other points of view.

INNATE ABILITY

The question of innate ability calls for no extended discussion, however, for many specialized volumes have gone into the matter thoroughly. From such sources the conclusion seems clear that the range of individual ability within any large racial group is much greater than any possible variation between two racial groups—that every race contains countless more persons who *could* attain high levels of achievement than *do*. Obviously those who do rise have ability, but since many others with equal ability never make the effort, the variable must apparently be sought in some other condition.

OTHER CHILDHOOD FACTORS

What, then, may be said about other childhood factors as determining personality? Negro youth are after all, and first of all, individuals; each is a different and complex person. Health, stature, mental ability, emotional type, social position within the family, childhood crisis experiences, and many other considerations enter into a full explanation of any Negro boys or girl's personality.

For example, in the case of Chester cited above, it was apparent that his superior mental ability (I.Q. 113) and his limited physical prowess had much to do with his responding to middle- rather than lower-class patterns for his satisfactions. Indeed, his early feeling of physical inferiority underlies his later aggressive tendencies and his extreme desire to succeed; his father often complained, "Why every kid in the neighborhood used to run over him, and he wouldn't fight back." As some success came to him, his confidence mounted. "Don't get the idea that I am inferior," he said to an interviewer. "I am far from it for I believe that I can fill any qualifications or equal any of the average boys, white or black, my age, physically, mentally, or any other way."

In contrast with the course of Chester's personality, his brother, Sidney, early established himself as a prize fighter, in spite of any influence his mother could exert to the contrary. What, in the last analysis, accounts for the radically different social outcome of these two boys? It cannot be the race factor, for they share this condition. Is it their difference in physique and mental ability, the variation in balance of their glandular functions, the different ways in which the family tensions and relationships define their respective roles, the different incentives and pressures which school and vocational groups place upon them?

The answer is that all of these factors and more must be considered in the cases of individual Negro youth before a conclusion can be reached. The field investigators did examine all of these factors in interpreting the data. But in this volume, which is intended to show how the lot of Negro youth differs from that of white youth, emphasis is placed upon the two conditions which are most typical of Negro youth: their membership in a race which American society has seen fit to subordinate; and their membership, by and large, in the lowest social class. The importance of other factors which might appear in the life of any youth are here acknowledged, but because of the purpose of this volume less space is given to a direct discussion of them.

CONCLUSION

Some Negro youth do participate in the American dream. In a few cases it is because their parents have shielded them from the cruder ways of the masses and have surrounded them with every expectancy of success. Other Negro youth meet a mixture of incentives, but those related to respectability win out because of the personal influence of a relative, a teacher, or some other friend with prestige. Still others are pushed upward by innate ability and by childhood experiences only indirectly connected with color or class.

The mass of Negro youth, however, are isolated from the American dream—isolated by economic conditions which seem to make personal striving futile and by a lack of participation in a culture of "respectability." They are more responsive to the colorful satisfactions of good times here and now, to sex indulgence, and to other free-and-easy behavior which parents do not or cannot suppress and which the example of other youth incites. True, many of these youth are relaxed, free of tensions, seldom bothered by neuroses, close to nature, even able to appreciate a good sunset or a drenching rain. But, since many of them do not live for the morrow, do not grind away at school subjects, do not feel conscience-stricken if they are late for work some morning, do not run from a good fight on Saturday night, they are judged by white middle-class society as shiftless, irresponsible, aggressive. These youth are called "no-count" by a society which isolates them from a way of living which it counts as all-important. Thus, low wages or none at all, exclusion from many types of work, and, more subtly, exclusion from the rewards and recognition which would make persons socially restrained and ambitious have held Negro youth apart. No one intends it so. Few understand the intimate cultural processes at work, but all feel free to criticize the finished product. In the next chapter this isolated group will be studied more intensively.

CHAPTER IV

THOSE WHO HAVE BEEN ISOLATED FROM THE AMERICAN DREAM

SELMA HALE of Greene County, Georgia, who wished for a decent house, enough to eat, and a few clothes, has an idea of a better way of living, but she has been prevented from attaining it. It would be natural for her, seeing the disparity between her aspirations and her achievement, to develop a sense of frustration and to find satisfaction in less desirable but more easily attainable ways. She says:

> I'd like to have a house that don't leak, a house with no leaks in it anywhere. I wants a comfortable house, a house you won't freeze in in winter. I'd like to have nice things in the house, nice furniture so you could be comfortable. I'd like for it to have smooth floors, not big loose planks.

> By being well cared for, I meant to have enough to eat. To have something to eat every day. Lots of days we don't have nothing to eat. It must be nice to have enough to eat every day . . . I'd like to have some clothes, too, like other girls.

THOSE WHO ASPIRE BUT CANNOT ACHIEVE

The field studies indicated that there was no better place to study frustration of this type than in the small northern community. Here the tradition of liberalism in race relations has given Negro youth an expectation of freedom in community life. In their childhood experiences they are accepted in the churches, in the schools, and on the playgrounds. Some are favored by white teachers who, recognizing their traditional handicap, give them special encouragement. Service clubs allocate part of their educational funds to Negro youth. Honors in athletics, in class offices, and in scholastic attainment also come their way. Responding to these incentives, the boy or girl feels no isolation and expects his good fortune to continue. He has already experienced some of the blessings of the American dream.

Sad, therefore, is the awakening which comes to many of these youth when, upon graduation from high school, they find that the communities did not really mean to be liberal, that, although a service club would help a Negro boy to complete his high school course, its members would not give him a job after his schooling was over. Even before graduation day the lines of participation had been drawn and his social contacts were limited largely to other Negroes in the community, and in many small towns there are too few of them to provide any satisfactory kind of society. Unless he could manage to continue his education and settle in a larger community, his prospect of success was exceedingly slight.

Harry X. had such experiences. As a boy, he included among his acquaintances and friends the leading citizens of his small northern community. His own home life, though limited by low income, was based upon the better patterns of living in the community. His sister was married with the same ceremony as a white girl, and her attendants wore the same kind of clothes as those at a middle-class white wedding.

To Harry all of this now seems a bit ironic. Forced by the financial needs of his family to remain in his small community, he discovered that there was no job to be had as a clerk in a grocery store, a reporter on the town newspaper, a bookkeeper in the bank, or a supervisor at the playground. Limited to the economic roles of bootblack or janitor, the high aspirations which his high school honors had stimulated were scaled downward sharply.

Soured in his outlook on life by having his full participation in the American dream changed to an almost complete isolation from it, he developed compensatory personality traits. Instead of taking the opportunities still open to him and resolving to get a higher education when he could, he assumed that the world was against him and developed real adeptness in excusing himself from any responsibility for his plight. To make a living he engaged in various illegal activities entirely out of keeping with his former way of life; in interracial matters he was bitter and distrustful, thus depriving himself of his former white friends. Later, while working as a WPA janitor, he reacted with strong emotion to suggestions from foremen and interpreted any criticisms as a further proof of racial prejudice. His personal ambition was thus replaced by an adjustment at a low social and economic level, and his former ability to criticize himself by a tendency to preserve his self-respect through shifting all blame.

The psychological principle involved in such conduct is no more complicated than that which explains the reaction of the child who is offered a piece of candy, only to have it jerked away as he reaches for it. It is the same principle which explains the frustration of white youth who, after having been reared in the tradition of the American dream, find that unemployment, military service, or some other factor has interrupted their march upward. The difference between the frustration of white and Negro youth is not in the psychological processes involved, but in the fact that for the Negro racial discrimination is added to all of the other forms of barriers encountered by youth.

THOSE WHO DO NOT ASPIRE

A less subtle but more effective and permanent form of isolation is experienced by another group of Negro youth who have never known what the white world expects of them. High percentages of Negro youth in all large communities and in many small ones have never understood the American ideal, let alone adopted it as a personal goal. Although from casual observation or an infrequent visit to the movies they may have acquired a vague notion of how the other half lives, these conventional patterns from the "upper world" are so far removed from their own firsthand observations that they have little reality or functional value.

For example, the cotton field comes to the very door of Joe D.'s home but that means poverty, not wealth. No crop was planted last year and the white landlord—not Joe's parents—cashed the government's check for soil conservation. Joe's family is destitute. There are plenty of children but no place for them to sleep, not enough food to go around. The house has no screens; the water supply is a hole in the ground, a bucket, and a rope; there is no toilet either inside the house or outside. Fuel has to be gathered wherever it can be found and there is only one kerosene lamp on the place. Although frequently ill, none of the children has received a doctor's care, none has visited a dentist.

Joe, now 10 years old, will go to the country school—when he feels like it—for another year or two. From his associates he will learn how to fight; he will also learn that girls are for sex satisfaction, but he will hear little about marriage. He will work at odd jobs and spend his dollar in a crap game or for cheap liquor. He will get religion at the summer revival, lose it the next day.

Tired of hanging around home and with no job or place of his own, he will wander to the city. He will make a little money as a bootblack on Saturdays, learn how to be a "policy writer," graduate to the hold-up game, survive several bad liquor fights, end up in prison. Or he will get a common laborer's job that will last for a month or two. His children

—even if he knows who they are—will receive little parental guidance and, left to the devices of the neighborhood gang, will become precocious in fighting, stealing, and sex. Doing well in school or attending at all after the sixth grade will be out of the question for them.

Like Elmer Gantry, Joe may combine more than his share of "sinful" traits, but the conditions which his life history illustrates are prevalent in Negro life. Rural and urban, northern and southern, a higher ratio of the Negro population than of any other group must work to support itself. Furthermore, whenever one dips for a statistical sample, he finds more Negroes working for starvation pay, more partially employed, more applying for relief, more engaged in disagreeable low-status tasks than any other racial or national group. Of every 1,000 Negro women who work, 588 are domestics as compared with 141 white women, and 233 are farm laborers as compared with 24 white women. Of every 1,000 Negro men who work, 317 are common laborers as compared with 141 white men, 100 are sharecroppers as compared with 10 white men, and 193 are farm laborers as compared with 84 white men. Though Negroes constitute one-half of the population of Mississippi, in 1930 only 175 of them in the entire state had found clerical employment.

In the country, Negroes of the lower class—which, as we have seen, includes most of the colored population—live in unsanitary shacks; if they move to the city, they inhabit broken-down tenements on neglected streets, congested and garnished by accumulated wastes, and located in the dreariest residential sections. Since the art of living can be practiced well only when external circumstances are tolerably favorable, statistics on Negro health, though showing improvement, are still on the gloomy side. Negro youth are born at a faster rate, are ill more frequently, and die more quickly than youth of any other group. The tuberculosis mortality rates among Negro youth are over seven times as great as among white. Deaths from childbirth, pneumonia, food poisoning, and cerebral hemorrhage are well above the general average in number.

What is the meaning of this complex of facts about Negro youth leading all others in poor housing, poor health, illiteracy, illegitimacy, delinquency, violent crime, desertion, dependency, and other indices of what the general community considers lower-class conditions? Simply that the majority in each new generation of Negro youth are still bound by the unfavorable physical conditions and low social standards under which their ancestors were placed with the dissolution of slavery and they are effectively prevented from rising to a better way of living. True, the race has its middle- and upper-class representatives, but their number is so small as to be a narrow peak on a pyramid of poverty and social disorganization.

Why is a boy from the Negro masses apt to be careless, without ambition, uncouth, immoral, even criminal? For the answer we may look to his associates and to the place from which he comes. His culture provides no incentives for acquiring bathtubs, college degrees, recognition in *Who's Who*, a home of his own on a respectable street, a sedate family life. Without incentives and without the example of others, people do not strive, may not even use to advantage what they do have. This reaction is not a matter of race but of cultural sanctions and of human nature.

In the customs governing sex behavior, the isolation of Negroes from the general culture is easily observable. It is one thing to know what the accepted standards are and then to violate them—such infringements are not uncommon in any class—but it is quite another thing to have no conception of such standards. In a group of ten boys in Chicago, all separated from their own parents and living a footloose existence, the investigator found an almost complete absence of inhibition in their reporting of sex relations. These boys were not "naturally" immoral because they were Negroes, as white judgments so often indicate; they merely had never known other standards. They reported their sex behavior, which a middle-class schoolteacher would condemn as immoral, as freely and unemotionally as they did their employment records or their love of swimming. With them some forms of sex behavior were taboo, and they had received some warnings and instruction from friends, but their sex behavior would indicate that they were thoroughly isolated from accepted middle-class standards.

Similar isolation is common in other types of behavior. Many colored youth have never known family life of the traditional pattern. Eating at the dining table as a family group is outside their experience. Having the same "father" for a period of years is unknown to many Negro boys and girls because the mating relations of their parents shift so frequently.

These ways of living are in part a continuation of the common practices of slavery. Two generations is too short a time to be freed from a social system in which the lower-caste group was regarded as innately inferior and consequently incapable of achieving the white man's standards of personal conduct and family life.

Throughout the long history of slavery the group on top developed the characteristic attitude of regarding the group underneath as less deserving and less able. In general, people tend to live up to what is expected of them. If not much is expected, then there is not very much "living up to" to do. Negro slaves were good slaves if they worked hard, kept their fights to themselves, and had plenty of children. Some house servants were expected to take on more subtle ways, and they did. And the small number of freed Negroes who moved North were expected to play a more refined role, and they did. But the bulk of the slaves, those who worked in the fields, had simple demands made of them and they were left to their own devices regarding personal conduct and family life. From the point of view of the white man, those devices often showed a lack of moral sense, and even today the white community comments on the immorality of Negro youth.

The influences of slavery were not lost with emancipation, but they are diminishing and new forces are taking their place. Nevertheless, this is still a transition period, and for a time unmorality (not immorality, which is possible only when standards are known and ignored) will allow many Negro youth to become adjusted to habits of living which some white critics do not approve. Obviously the problem is to find techniques whereby more and more Negro youth can participate in a cultural heritage comparable to that of white youth. As the community itself increasingly regards Negro youth as able and worth while, and as subtle ways are found of introducing certain cultural patterns into the early experience of Negro youth through rewards or punishments, then we can expect Negro youth to respond in the same way as white youth similarly treated.

Of course, this more extreme degree of isolation which we have been discussing is not entirely limited to colored youth. Clifford R. Shaw and Henry D. McKay have investigated gangs of white boys in the West Madison district of Chicago, for whom jack-rolling, shop-lifting, and other forms of delinquency are more familiar than regular school attendance, Boy Scout membership, and summer vacations in the country. These boys have their own culture to which they respond. But the society which is in charge of the courts, the churches, and other institutions of the community does not approve of this culture and imprisons those who follow its pattern.

Although many white youth are reared in such situations, the relative proportion of Negro youth is far higher. Their rates of delinquency, of disease, of violent death, of dependency, of poor housing conditions, and of many other indices all point to the socio-psychological factor (which is more important than the physical one) that more Negro youth than white are born into a culture set apart.

Another type of isolation which holds Negro youth apart is the obvious factor of castelike restrictions. The nature of the discriminations will not be reviewed in this volume, but rather we shall consider the reactions of Negro youth to them. Because these caste barriers influence so many aspects of personality adjustment, the following chapter will be devoted to their consideration.

CHAPTER V

LEARNING HOW TO BE BLACK IN A WHITE WORLD

WHITE CHILDREN in the United States take many things for granted. Very early in life they learn, without being told in so many words, that they are as good as or better than any other people in the world and that they live in a land especially blessed.

On the other hand, American children who are born with Negroid features have to learn a different conception of themselves and of their opportunities. They may thrill to patriotic music, respond to stirring historical accounts of the nation's founding, and take pride in the country's rapid growth, in the development of its great cities, and in its preparation for defense, but that pride is often tainted by the realization that these great achievements really belong to the white man's world. The Negro boy or girl is inclined to feel that though a native, he is still a foreigner. Though he helped create these wonders he cannot show them off as "mine." Though he may rise to a high position within his own group, he must always be on guard lest his color bring embarrassment or outright insult.

With some youth, learning how to be a Negro in a predominantly white world is not a difficult task, while to others, learning how to preserve self-respect and acquire ambition to rise while belonging to a subordinate group takes on the proportions of a personal crisis. No one pattern of adjustment or rebellion will describe all cases. The biological nature of the individual has an effect upon his interracial behavior, and his earliest interracial contacts are

often crucial in defining his later mode of response. His home training in racial attitudes is important; his schooling, his occupation, his membership in social groups, and many other factors enter into a full account of a particular child's reaction to his membership in a minority racial group.

Curiously, however, although the determining factors in any given case are numerous, several patterns of personality adjustment to racial status have become almost standardized among Negro youth. These patterns are a part of Negro culture and are transmitted like any other culture patterns. The standardization is never complete, for new patterns or new combinations come into use; but the repetition is sufficiently frequent to make their description of value. There are two types of standardization. The first is in the ways Negro youth learn that they belong to a group set apart, and the second is in what they do about it.

LEARNING THAT THEY ARE SET APART

Facts about racial status like facts about sex are generally picked up here and there rather than from systematic study. From parents, playmates, and white persons Negro children gradually or suddenly come to a realization that they are regarded as different by the white community.

Some youth learn what it means to be Negro through a crisis experience as was true of the boy who reported:

> A white man yanked me off a streetcar because I got on ahead of a white woman. He shook me good and tore my clothes. I walked home crying, knowing that my father would do something about it. (But his father could do no more than remark, "You should have known better.")

Some Negro youth take over the attitudes of their parents and grandparents who have accepted the unequal status of the races as natural and inevitable. This was true of the 14-year-old boy who in answer to questions about race relations replied that "white people treat colored people all right," or, "as good as they ought to." One boy reported that when he lived in North Carolina his parents had always taught him and his brothers and sisters

> to do as we were told, be as courteous as possible to white people, don't talk back to them, and do your work as well as possible. They said "niggers" that are liked by white people are those who don't give any trouble and don't ask for much.

These illustrations of ways in which Negro youth learn that they are a group set apart are taken from Frazier's *Negro Youth at the Crossways*. After citing these two cases the author comments: "Usually the parents, even those with a southern background, do not indoctrinate their children with such patently servile attitudes. . . . The instructions to the children concerning the avoidance of trouble with whites ranges from general admonitions about keeping away from 'white places because colored aren't allowed' to rather detailed techniques, sometimes accompanied by generalizations on the white man's character."

Since in his two chapters, "The Role of the Family," and "Neighborhood Contacts," Frazier goes thoroughly into the first question of the ways in which Negro youth learn of their status, we shall proceed to the second question as to what Negro youth do about it after they have learned of their unequal position. All of the authors of the various volumes in the series report standard patterns which the Negro community has worked out for coping with social inequality. Since these folkways enter the individual's experience as his own mode of adjustment, their importance in a study of personality development is apparent.

MAKING ADJUSTMENTS TO CASTELIKE STATUS

Learning that one is Negro is one thing; knowing what to do about it is another. The patterned ways of adjusting to their minority status which we shall now consider reveal how intimately the culture of discrimination is related to the personality adjustment of Negro youth. The first way of meeting the problem is an attempt to avoid it.

DODGING CASTELIKE BARRIERS

One method of avoiding the unpleasantness of the castelike situation is to escape from it altogether by "passing over."

Passing Over

No one knows exactly how many Negro youth have taken the final step of complete identification with white society, for obviously the secret is guarded. The investigators in this study were certain that the proportion was very small, but that there were enough cases to justify listing this way out as one of the possible reactions. We may, therefore, consider that one response to being a Negro is, paradoxically, *not to be one.* At first glance this seems to be an easy solution for those of light skin. Actually it is one of the most difficult kinds of adjustment. Knowing the punishment which the white caste would mete out were the deceit uncovered, the individual is forever insecure.

Furthermore, the emotional amputation involved in most cases creates a difficult situation. The Negro who "passes" must sever the close bonds with colored friends and relatives which have developed over a period of years. A sense of guilt is very likely to accompany such a renunciation, especially during a period of crisis.

For example, the brother and sister of a prominent Negro religious leader chose to "pass over" as their solution of the race problem. All went nicely in their contacts in the white world until their Negro mother became critically ill. Their inability to visit her and later to attend the funeral, because of fear of detection, produced such feelings of guilt and isolation that the rewards of the "new world" were questionable gains.

As might be expected, the "passing over" pattern is not only infrequent but is also limited almost entirely to urban communities where anonymous living makes it easier for one to change social roles without detection. Even in cities, however, the shift probably occurs very seldom.

In a modified form of the pattern, the Negro makes no pretense of concealing his racial identity when he is with his own people, but for the sake of greater freedom, he passes for white temporarily whenever he cares to do so. Only by mingling with a lynching mob as though he were white could Walter White have secured the intimate facts for his book on lynching. Later, while he was lobbying for a federal antilynching bill, he lived in a fashionable hotel in Washington until his picture appeared on the cover of *Time*. Walter White's colored friends do not object to his playing a dual role because they know he is not trying to become a white person. He is merely increasing his effectiveness as a race leader by having greater freedom of movement.

Upper-Class Complacency

A much more common pattern for avoiding the unpleasantness of the caste situation may be seen among some middle- and upper-class Negroes who studiously avoid contacts with white groups.

When a Negro living in Washington, D.C., invited a white friend to accompany him to a social affair given by upper-class Negroes, he was rebuked privately for bringing the white man along. The group was composed of self-satisfied upper-class persons who welcomed no intruders from the white world.

There was evidence in the field studies that middle- and upper-class Negroes are often more preoccupied with their own social climbing than with forming social contacts across racial lines. The Negro professional or businessman who has built up a clientele within his own race, who has a well-organized family life, who lives in a desirable neighborhood, and who is held in high esteem by the "better class" people of his community may, in fact, be relatively unaffected by the racial question.

It is the white man who attributes unhappiness to such a person and a desire to take "the next logical step" of becoming assimilated by white society. Racial conceit has no doubt entered into the white man's fear that the ambitious Negro has intermarriage with white persons as his ultimate goal. On the contrary, the ambitious Negro has high position in his own society as his objective. Too free participation across the racial line would be the easiest way of slipping socially within his own group.

One should not infer that the Negro who has attained high standing in his own circle is entirely free of conflict and frustration. He may still suffer from emotional scars left by earlier experiences in his upward climb. Or he may still be subject to humiliating interracial experiences. Even though they occur in relations such as travel, recreation, and hotel living, they are, nevertheless, signs of a caste position which is a blunt reminder to him that in spite of his class superiority[1] he is still a member of a lower caste.[2]

To find a desirable place to live is an especially acute aspect of the adjustment problem for the socially ambitious Negro. An upper-class family wishing to escape the congestion of the poorer areas and to find a "high class" neighborhood in which to rear children often moves to the periphery

---

[1] To many sensitive Negroes the coming of the automobile has been a second emancipation because through its use they can avoid the most conspicuous forms of Jim-Crowism on busses, streetcars, and trains.

[2] After reading this section, President Malcolm S. MacLean of Hampton Institute commented: "One of the most sensitive spots I have found is in discrimination in medical care and hospitalization. Because illness heightens emotional sensitivity and lowers one's guards and self-control, even the most hardened Negro is likely to go to pieces when the insults to which he is inured in health occur in sickness."

of the "black belt." The periphery then becomes the firing line between white defenders and colored invaders of an area in transition. This and similar adjustment problems disturb the complacency of upper-class Negroes. Some make the best of it; others join or lead protest movements against racial discrimination.

Negro youth resent still more such caste barriers as limitations in employment which keep them from rising to higher standards of social living. True, the doctor, the undertaker, or the schoolteacher may work so completely with members of his own race that for days at a time he can avoid contacts with white persons if he chooses to do so, and the larger Negro communities are also developing business and entertainment enterprises to such an extent that many who live there can obtain all services without going to white establishments.

Although the business and professional opportunities involved in serving the Negro population may support a few individuals, they provide a meager basis for the development of a strong middle- or upper-class group. Furthermore, many of the opportunities that do exist within the Negro community have been taken over by white businessmen or by chain stores which can readily finance new enterprises.

The establishment of a separate economy for Negroes which would furnish an independent basis for their social development was proposed in an earlier day as a cure-all solution, but is now recognized to be as impossible of achievement as the establishment of a separate relief economy for the unemployed. Therefore, if Negroes are to have a fair chance to achieve a financial basis for upper-class social living, present inequalities based on race alone must be corrected. The desire of Negro youth is not for admission to white society, but for a chance to support a way of living which would mark anyone, white or colored, as belonging to a culturally superior group.

Other Means of Escape

It will easily be seen that fairly complete avoidance of caste barriers is possible only to those who can "pass over" and to the upper economic groups in the Negro community. Avoidance is far more difficult for other Negro individuals and classes. Economic isolation is possible for only a relatively few professional men and businessmen; the great majority of employed Negro youth must continue to work for white persons and to ride on streetcars and busses. There are, it is true, such other patterns of avoidance as ordering merchandise by catalogue, arranging for Pullman reservations by telephone, or traveling by car to avoid embarrassment of exclusion from sleeper and hotel accommodations, enjoying home entertainment instead of going to movies where only balcony seats are available, and attending all-colored churches, sports events, and celebrations. It is only by such withdrawal that most sensitive Negroes can avoid wounding contacts.

There is, of course, the rare instance of the all-Negro community. Of one such community, Mound Bayou, Mississippi, a Negro youth said to an interviewer:

> I don't believe in whites and colored mixing together. That's why I likes Mound Bayou, you don't have to mix with the white folks. Everything is run by colored people. . . . Colored folks feel better when they don't have white folks around.

This is not a common attitude, for the community is not typical, but it illustrates another step in the range of reactions to interracial problems.

DEFENDING THE RACE

Quite unlike the pattern followed by those who avoid the caste situation is the more common pattern of defending "the race," which is followed by Negroes in all classes of society, and is especially typical of the "race leader."

The Race Leader

At a Negro debutante's party racial discrimination does not enter the minds of most of the guests. However, for at least one person present at many such gatherings, race relations are of paramount importance. He is the "race leader"—the middle- or upper-class Negro whose profession it is to champion the rights of the colored masses. He does not talk "business" during a party but the next morning takes up the cudgels again by organizing boycotts, editing a journal devoted to the emancipation of the masses, or inducing white friends to write to members of Congress. His business as race journalist or race leader is sufficiently profitable to give him middle- or upper-class standing while he is fighting for the masses.

When a white audience hears race leader Dr. D., president of a Negro college, decry the hardships of the Negro race, it is moved to pity for the plight of the Negro. In his own private life, however, Dr. D. has nothing to do with the masses. He and his family occupy a large house, employ three servants, including a chauffeur, and in their own drawing room discuss politics, literature, travel, and music more frequently than race relations. They rear their own children in such a way as to protect them not only from unpleasant racial experiences, but also from contact with the masses of their own race.

Race leadership has become for Dr. D. a professional pursuit. There are relatively few such positions in the Negro community, but they constitute an especially interesting pattern because of their mixture of class and caste factors.

"I Want to Be Black"

A somewhat similar but less professionalized reaction than that of the race leader is the racial patriotism of the persons who seek to protect their own egos by speaking out boldly in defense of the group of which they are members.

I don't care if I am the blackest one. . . . I wouldn't be yellah for nothin'. If I was born again I'd want to be just as black, if anything, a little blacker. . . . All niggahs are supposed to be black. . . . I don't like yellah niggahs, 'cause they think they're so damn cute.

. . . .

Of course you may think I'm crazy, but I'm proud I'm a Negro. I won't say that I would like to change, because I wouldn't.

. . . .

I am bursting over with race pride but I try to keep it from blinding me. I think of my race as my big family and my own parents, relatives, and my own little groups as within that big family, and all races as just one great big family.

Where the race leader has made a profession of his group loyalty, the persons quoted above are merely expressing their personal feelings on interracial matters. Yet even their expressions of racial pride are not always to be taken literally. The person of dark pigmentation cannot conceal his racial identity and must find some way to preserve his pride while occupying a subordinate status. One way of doing this is to affirm that the apparent handicap is really a desirable quality. Although the person may not express outright favor for Negroidness, he at least resents any connotation of inferiority when his color or race is mentioned.

This reaction may involve contradictory ambivalent attitudes: some youth really hate their Negroidness because of the handicaps it brings them; and yet, because these youth dare not express this hatred, they cover their feelings by going to the other extreme of praising all that is Negroid. Such a conflict of emotions produces tensions which may affect the individual's occupational and social adjustment generally.

STRIKING BACK

Closely related to the pattern of defending the race is that of striking back at white affronts, either real or imagined. This pattern is much more common than might ordinarily be supposed.

Aggressive Behavior

Outright aggression against white persons is more the privilege of Negro children than of grownups because lynchings, the police, and job losses are constant threats to the mature Negro who veers too far from his traditional role in the local community. Some of the less inhibited behavior of children who have rebelled against constraint is illustrated by the following case excerpts:

> Jimmy is a fighter. He ain't scared of nobody. He'll call white children names quick as not.
>
> . . . .
>
> Once a white girl deliberately bumped into me, and I flew into her. An older woman got out of her car and grabbed me. It was a good thing, too, because the policeman was coming. She took me on home.
>
> . . . .
>
> Once he threatened to beat up two white boys who had formed the habit of calling him "nigger" whenever he rode by them on his bicycle. He did not have any trouble from then on. Another time he answered back a white boy who had made a remark he did not like. The white boy came after him as if to start a fight but he stood his ground with a flashlight as a weapon. Again he was able to call a white boy's bluff.
>
> . . . .
>
> Julia feels that she is rejected—by her mother because she is the darkest of all the children, by whites because she is a "nigger." She adjusts to her rejection by aggressive behavior. In the theater she is a trouble-maker—"Sometimes I lean over the banister and spit down on them ol' white people's head." Repeatedly she says, "I hate white people!" When a white woman called her a nigger, she threatened to beat the woman. Yet she has had a few pleasant experiences with whites.

All of the field studies reported a freer, more aggressive type of behavior among lower-class children than in middle- and upper-class circles. In many lower-class neighborhoods, loud talk, threats, and fights between white and colored boys are not uncommon. But as children grow older, they meet a more rigid set of attitudes which makes interracial fighting a serious offense, punishable by law or by vigilante action. The seriousness of such behavior when a Negro boy reaches work age is seen in the following instance:

> When Simmons was struck by his white employer, he knocked the white man down and then ran. He escaped pursuing whites, but that night the sheriff arrested him. Simmons' father protested. "Some white man hit my boy." Said the sheriff, "You mean, yore boy hit a *white* man!"

Although such community threats cause Negro youth to inhibit their aggressive behavior as they grow older, some youth revert to it when provoked, even though grave consequences may follow. Such occasional outbursts of violence among rural Negroes, who are supposed to "stay in their place," were reported by Johnson:

> Some white men fool around with Negro women, and nigger men are too scared to do anything. Course once in a while niggers kill 'em up. Then they got to take to the bushes and go ahead. If they ketch him, they just hang him to a bridge.

In addition to occasional outbursts in interracial relations, violence within their own society is not uncommon at the lower levels of Negro society. Knife fighting and drunken brawls are not as prevalent as some white critics suppose, nor are they rare occurrences.

The Negro upper classes look down upon such behavior as crude and undignified. Just as middle- or upper-class white people do not indulge in fist fights, riots, or brawls, but rather settle their disputes through court action, so similar levels in Negro society have their nonviolent ways of avoiding, absorbing, or settling interpersonal and interracial problems.

There are, however, rare instances of aggression outside of lower-class groups. Since such behavior is contrary to the common culture of the upper groups, it may be assumed to represent a personality maladjustment. A post-office employee in Chicago, whose middle-class decorum should have prevented him from fist fighting, did fight white workers whenever he overheard or imagined he overheard a slurring remark about him. His extreme sensitiveness and emotional outbursts led to his dismissal.

This case is exceptional. The customary pattern in middle- and upper-class circles is not aggressive revolt against but adjustment to interracial conditions. Because barriers are experienced by all Negroes, they are seldom taken by any one individual as a personal insult. In an objective manner, upper-class Negroes discuss the status of their caste and support efforts for its improvement, but their immediate, personal concern is with their own status within the Negro group. The girl of 17 is much more worried about her failure to receive an invitation to a debutante's party than about the passage of the "antilynch bill" in Congress. That is to say, so matters appear on the surface.

Actually, almost no upper-class Negro is free of inner conflict about his caste status. His apparent objectivity covers up inner dread of and resentment about humiliating experiences. The upper-class Negro man, especially when accompanied by his fiancée or his wife, is not completely at ease until the evening's entertainment or the day's trip is over and nothing embarrassing has happened. True, the Negro girl mentioned, like all debutantes, is living gloriously for the moment, but discussions of race relations are also a frequent part of her experience. She cannot escape the problems of her minority group permanently, and she knows it.

Vicarious Aggression

Class status does not have as much to do with a safer type of aggression common among Negro youth, namely, vicarious aggression. Such statements as the following reflect feelings which are not limited to any one group within the Negro community, but are expressed in different ways at all social levels:

> The night he [Joe Louis] lost was a sad one. . . . I'll always believe he was doped. . . . You can't beat a Negro doing anything if you give him an equal break.
>
> . . . .
>
> Well, for years whites have kicked Negroes about and I'm happy somebody came along who could kick the stuffings out of the toughest "hombres" the whites could put up against him.
>
> . . . .
>
> I've thrilled at every damned "peck" he knocked over.
>
> . . . .
>
> I was hitting every blow with him, and taking with him those he got.

Joe Louis is a popular hero of Negro youth not only because of the honors he has received but also because of his symbolic value as a successful aggressor against white domination. The youth just quoted feel vicarious satisfaction every time Louis downs a white foe.

Identification with a hero is not the only attitude of Negro youth toward Joe Louis, however, for as the following reactions indicate, class attitudes again assert themselves in the reactions of upper-class Negroes toward the social and educational position which Joe Louis represents.

> Outside of fighting, I think he is a laughing stock. It is too bad he is so ignorant.
>
> . . . .
>
> I listen to his fights, but I wish he wouldn't talk on the radio. He's dumb, but he's a great fighter. He can lick any white fighter.
>
> . . . .
>
> I think people who go around beating up other people are just ignorant. That doesn't help anything the least bit.

These statements show how caste and class considerations produced mixed reactions in the person.

Nevertheless, Joe Louis' victories have provided a safe type of aggression for many Negro youth who resent being dominated by a white world. The percentage of Negro-owned radios tuned in on a Joe Louis fight is very high, and, although some listeners have only a casual interest, many gain real emotional satisfaction when a white man is knocked out.

Shifting the Blame

Since this vicarious aggression is common, it is not thought of as a form of personal maladjustment. Maladjustment is always relative to a situation, for if one has social approval he can engage in a type of emotionalism that would cause him to be thought of as abnormal if he were to do the same thing without group support.

But how does one account for the occasional Negro youth who acts without such group support, who revolts emotionally against restraint, and who shifts blame for his failure from personal weakness to caste barriers? The practical effects of thus expressing personal maladjustment in racial terms are seen in the experience of a former government administrator in Washington who tried to be liberal in granting employment to Negro applicants. Ordinarily he encountered no difficulty, but occasionally a Negro employee became highly sensitive to racial injustice and the administrator faced a difficult personnel problem. Although the employee's aggressive manner and demands for justice may have reflected a maladjustment which had little or nothing to do in the beginning with race relations, yet on the job it was expressed in these terms. If the white administrator criticized, demoted, or discharged the employee, or if he promoted a white man over him, the Negro shifted all blame away from his own personal inadequacy and viewed the problem solely as a matter of race prejudice. Furthermore, since race prejudice is in reality so often responsible for inequality in employment, his excuse seems plausible.

In leaving the subject of aggressive interracial conduct, it should be noted that patterns of physical aggression are limited rather closely to the lower classes, but that vicarious aggression and the tendency to make an excuse of color are to be found in all ranks of the Negro community. For a system of race relations which is neither a completely rigid caste arrangement nor a free, democratic form of intergroup association, this country has to a surprising degree been spared group outbreaks and individual aggression.

SERVILITY

Outwardly opposite from the aggressive pattern is that of servility, which has long been a common technique of survival for Negro personality.

The "White Man's Nigger"

Servility in the following illustrations is a studied device for getting what one wants but is not the only type of adjustment in which servility is expressed.

> To get along with whites let them think at all times that they are better than you are, that the white man is boss, and act as humble as possible.
>
> . . . .
>
> Treat white people courteous at all times and if necessary, do a little flattering and "coat-tail" kissing.
>
> . . . .
>
> All white people want, anyway, is to feel superior, and I'm the man to play their game. I don't care what they do or say, so long as they "kick in."
>
> . . . .
>
> A "good nigger" avoids all conflicts with whites and observes the taboos in detail. He (or she) must "act the monkey and coat-tail the whites." There must be outward acceptance of inferiority. The "good nigger" cheerfully accepts low wages, lack of opportunity, "bawlings out," and so on.

Unlike the pose of humility revealed in these quotations, servility may in many cases represent a genuine, thoroughgoing adjustment to servant status in which no trace of rebellion or complaint can be found. The individual gradually and unwittingly becomes adjusted to his status, or he is so successfully "born into a servant status" that not until outside influences intervene does he learn that another relationship might be possible, and this realization or desire may never come to him. Psychologically, his servant status has many compensations and does not of itself produce rebellion. Even during the Civil War, many servants accompanied their masters to the battlefield, not because they were forced to do so, but because such a close bond of loyalty had developed through years of service that this was the natural thing for them to do.

Similarly today, there are southern families in which the relationship between servant and employer is not so much a matter of wages and expedient behavior as of sentiment and loyalty. The work which many Negroes perform, particularly in domestic service, is complicated, and good performance brings reward in the form of approval from the employer and self-satisfaction on the part of the servant. A skilled cook who provides an elaborate dinner, a personal maid who is entrusted with confidences and responsibility, and a well-trained butler who knows the social amenities better than some of the guests who are being entertained have a sense of status which is often overlooked by the outsider. Unless the conditions of work are especially unpleasant or some leader in the community encourages complaint, adjustment to the servant role is customary.

On the other hand, the emotional going is not smooth in every case. One Negro who played the outward role of subserviency ("treat white people courteous at all times, and if necessary, do a little 'coat-tail' kissing") admitted privately, "I hate myself every time I say 'boss,' or 'coat-tail' a peckerwood."

When colored butlers and maids overhear "darky stories" at the dinner table there may be a deep resentment which white observers fail to notice. Some servants are so adept in concealing their true feelings that their employers either mistakenly think they "know their servants well" or admit that they are at a loss to know what is really on their minds. One employer who suspected communist interests on the part of his workers, said that he thought he would conceal a microphone in the servants' quarters to discover what they were really saying.

Although outward servility in Negro-white relations involves all of these subtleties, the field studies failed to show evidence that outward adjustment to subordinate status was not the customary reaction when the work situation required it and when it was a common pattern in the community.

"Clowning"

The jovial, clowning manner which incorrectly has become a stereotyped description of Negro personality does actually exist in some cases and for understandable reasons.

> So I don't mind trying and if you know how to flatter and "jive" white people, you can get farther than they expect "niggers" to go. I usually make a big joke of it and act the part of a clown. I generally get just what I'm after.

Frequently, clowning is a conscious technique designed to release tensions in interracial relations. Its effectiveness even in a formal courtroom setting is attested to by autobiographical statements in a number of cases.

But "acting the monkey" is also a means of releasing tensions within the individual himself, particularly in lower-class circles where the mores do not inhibit such expression. As one youth described the matter, "I know, being a 'nigger,' there are places I can't go and things I can't do. I make a joke of it and act the clown." The clowning reaction is sometimes used as a device for attracting attention in situations where the individual might otherwise be socially isolated. Loud talk attracts attention, even though it may be unfavorable attention.

Resignation

Accepting one's fate because there is nothing else to do, and bolstering one's pride with a religious interpretation of why things are as they are, was a common pattern of survival during slavery times and continues to be followed by many Negroes.

> I don't mind being jes' like Gawd made me. He made colored people, so I guess he must want 'em.
>
> . . . .
>
> I tell my children . . . when white folks don't treat you right, don't try to hit back. The Negro is weak . . . and the white man is in power. . . . we gotta leave it to Him to vengeance us. We're the underdog.

Resignation reduces wear and tear on one's personality. If the resigned soul can also contemplate a hereafter where justice, equality, and comfortable living abound, he is further aided in accepting the hardships of the present.

Seldom, however, does a person absorb all adverse conditions without protest. One parent in telling how she taught her children to face discrimination revealed an interesting combination of patterns, with the emphasis placed upon the acceptance of things as they are:

> I tell my children we just have to live together with all these whites, and they'd better learn how to get along. The best way is to have no fighting. Course, if a white child hits 'em, it's all right to hit back, but that may mean a lot of trouble. Whites have the upper hand. We just have to recognize that. Perhaps the Lord will straighten out things some day. I don't know. Meantime, we'd better get along with things as they are.

SUMMARY

The significant point regarding the patterns of behavior which have been described is that they have become standard ways of meeting interracial situations. These patterns are *in the culture*. From time to time the point has been made that certain reactions were more characteristic of lower- than upper-class youth or vice versa, but any attempt to separate them neatly upon such a basis would be arbitrary.

The particular pattern or combination of patterns which a given child may acquire is dependent upon many factors. Children unwittingly acquire some of their attitudes; they are taught others quite openly by parents who want to prepare them for what is ahead; and others they pick up for themselves through direct experiences with the other race. Learning how to be colored in a white world is a difficult task. Conditions of discrimination vary in different localities; they vary to some extent according to social class; and they often vary in their effect upon different personalities. Some youth make the adjustment easily, while for others the problem remains a constant source of conflict.

CHAPTER VI

HIGH VISIBILITY AND STATUS

RELATIONS BETWEEN the races have been the underlying problem throughout the last chapter. Now, it must be acknowledged that white attitudes subtly penetrate the colored world itself to determine in part how Negroes regard each other.

W. Lloyd Warner and his staff, who gave special attention to the color factor in Negro boys and girls' conceptions of themselves and in their regard for each other, went so far as to comment that color is possibly the most important single element that determines "for better or for worse" the development of Negro character. The other authors did not stress the point to this extent, but they all reported color prejudice or preference within Negro society and also acknowledged the preference which the white world often shows the individual who is less Negroid in appearance.

APPEARANCE AND SOCIAL SUCCESS

The importance of Negroidness (of which "high visibility" is only one criterion) in determining one's place in Negro society is not surprising when one realizes, as Warner points out, that in American society generally considerable emphasis is placed upon superficial appearance in getting ahead in the world. "Not only are the women urged to make themselves attractive but even the men are under pressure to 'spruce up.' Advertisements connecting vocational and social success or failure with sparkling teeth or sloppy socks, new shoes or baldness, are not at all unusual. . . . A society such as ours underlines the general human desire to look well. . . . What is true of American society as a whole is no less true of life in the Negro community. . . .

"The higher social value usually placed upon Caucasoid features has called into existence a sizable cosmetic industry. Skin bleaches, hair dressings, and hair straighteners are given considerable advertising even in those Negro newspapers that aggressively advocate more 'race solidarity' and deprecate intraracial color prejudice.[1] Appeals to 'race pride' are used, on the other hand, to sell colored dolls and children's books with handsome Negro characters, and there is much talk about the 'beautiful brownskin girls of our race.'

"What a Negro has to say about his color and that of other people, together with his response to color evaluations, may often furnish a direct key to all or most of his thoughts about himself and his very existence. Such evaluations somehow get involved in almost every incident in his life. . . . Nevertheless, there are individuals and whole groups for whom skin color is not the primary element in personality development, because there are other more potent factors in their circumstances."

COLOR VALUES

A Negro boy or girl often finds better opportunity for economic and social advancement if his color is light, but his race will keep him under surveillance for signs of race desertion. He must learn to get along with Negroes of his own class, and "if necessary, put himself out to win the acceptance of darker persons."

A brown-skinned Negro can be "all things to all men," shifting back and forth between the light-skinned groups and the dark-skinned groups. He can "affiliate with lighter people of higher status . . . or he can be a race leader along

---

[1] It would be incorrect to say that the cosmetic industry among Negroes is entirely a matter of racial sensitiveness. It is partly a matter simply of personal appearance as is the cosmetic industry supported by white customers. There is, nevertheless, a racial element, especially when one dealer advertises "select a powder one shade lighter than your complexion."

with darker people of high caste." His lot appears to be the happiest in the Negro society.

By dividing their group of 800 cases according to social class position, sex, place of birth, and degree of Negroidness, Warner and his staff described typical patterns of adjustment within each subcategory. They found that a woman of high social standing had the greatest difficulty in coping with the problem of black pigmentation, which is another way of saying that high social standing and blackness are incompatible.

The color factor was not found to be so important in the cases of men. If a dark-skinned man has compensatory qualities of exceptional ambition, intellectual ability, educational achievement, business success, and family background he can get along well even in purely social matters and his dark color will be no great handicap. There have been many Negro marriages in which dark but economically successful men have married light-skinned wives, but seldom does a black Negro woman wed a light-colored, Caucasian-featured Negro male. "Face value" is apparently of greater importance to a woman than to a man in colored as well as in white society.

At the lower social positions Warner and his staff found that adjustment to the color factor was less difficult. This is another way of saying that dark pigmentation and low status often go together. The dark-skinned janitor, ditch digger, or field hand can be quite at ease about his color, providing he is content to marry a girl of similar position and appearance. Even so, an occasional case of rebellion against color was found at the lower social levels.

In the other field reports, the authors may have stressed different aspects of the question but they arrived at essentially the same conclusion as did Warner, namely, that being Negro is one thing, but that being a very Negroid type of Negro is another. They also found that the attitudes of preference varied with the class position and sex of the persons in question.

Charles S. Johnson and his staff investigated indirectly through the use of attitude and color preference tests the color prejudice found within the Negro group. They found that in answer to such questions as "What boy do you like best," or "Who is the ugliest girl you know," there is a tendency either to attach unfavorable judgments to dark-skinned individuals, or to fill the unfavorable judgments by describing as "black" disliked individuals whose skin may actually be no darker than persons about whom they have a favorable judgment and describe as dark-brown. In either case a prejudice against dark pigmentation is revealed.

Not only do "black" persons fare poorly in social judgments but also Negroes who are "yellow" or "white" do not win favor as readily as those who are brown. Apparently the lightest shades are not favored because they suggest a complete identification with the white pattern and a desertion of the Negro racial type and the Negro social world. Wavy, not kinky hair, sharp rather than heavy facial features, and light-brown pigmentation represent the optimum when attention is given in social judgments to personal appearance.

In comparing the urban and rural studies the investigators found that more ado was made about color in the large than in the small communities. This was to be expected. If color is a status factor, it would count for most where the differences in status and the concern about status are the greatest. In many small communities, persons of all shades mingle freely and little preference is shown even in marriage. But in larger places and especially among the socially ambitious, color and physical appearance have to be taken along with other status factors in understanding the adjustment problems of Negro youth.

Color preference is only one aspect of the castelike relationship which was analyzed earlier and which will be summarized in the following chapter along with other factors which determine Negro youth's social status and consequently their attitudes about themselves. Although color prejudice within the Negro group is only one element among caste and class status factors discussed throughout this book, it was given special attention in this brief chapter because many readers who know something about race relations in general have missed this more subtle phase of the problem. These self-feelings and in-group prejudices reveal how even the inner circles of Negro society are not immune to the far-reaching effects of white superiority attitudes.

CHAPTER VII

WHAT DOES IT ALL ADD UP TO?

BRINGING TOGETHER conclusions from the complete series of studies of Negro youth and summarizing the findings of the entire project is not a simple task. The following summary will, nevertheless, group for the convenience of the reader the findings of staff members who set out to see what being Negro has to do with youth's adjustment. Since the generalizations will be stated without the usual "ifs and ands" and modifications, they should be considered by the research worker more as hypotheses worthy of trial in a program of action than as hard and fast conclusions to be accepted as proved once and for all. The more obvious facts about Negro-white relations will not be repeated here, but only those findings concerning the personality adjustment of Negro youth which might be assumed to give the general reader insights which he has not previously had.

LISTING THE FINDINGS

When the area directors were asked to list what they considered to be the principal findings in the research, they stressed different points, but in general reached agreement on what they considered basic. Allison Davis listed the essential factors in Negro youth's adjustment as follows:[1]

1. Within the Negro society, "standards" of behavior differ radically according to social classes.

---

[1] Obviously, these lists of points do not represent the authors' full or final interpretation of what it means to be born a Negro. For their more complete statements the separate volumes of the authors should be consulted.

2. The resulting differences in the training of the child and adolescent are so great that one cannot speak of "the problems" or "the characteristics" of "the *Negro* child." One must speak first in terms of the social class training of the child, and only secondarily of his caste training.

3. In brief, the types of social adjustment of Negroes to their caste restrictions differ according to a complex of variables, the most important of which are social class, age, and sex. (Color is, of course, included in the class variable.)

4. The types of personalities found among Negro adolescents seem to be explainable primarily in terms of early family and class training. While there is no doubt that his caste position presents major adjustment problems to a Negro child of any class, these problems are not as recurrent and character forming as those of family relationships and class relationships.

5. There are, however, many psychological (as well as social, economic, and political) disabilities of the lower-caste youth and his family. The downward pressure of the white caste makes an overwhelming proportion of Negroes lower class in their social and economic traits. This lower-class society in which most Negro children live does not offer a child rewards for economic, educational, and social effort of a severe kind, nor does it punish him for sexual and aggressive indulgence. Like white lower-class children, Negro lower-class children are motivated along lines quite different from middle-class children. The important point is that there are relatively so many more lower-class colored children than white in the South.

6. An even clearer example of the effect of caste upon the child's motivation is in education. Since the white society arbitrarily excludes Negroes from almost all white-collar, skilled, and professional work, the colored child has little stimulus to work hard during high school. He knows that the white society, which *is* the business world, offers him

no reward for the long work and renunciation which study requires. His only hope is to join the relatively small number of Negro physicians and teachers, who are maintained by the working of the caste system itself. If there is one consistent response from colored students, it is that they place little value upon doing well in school. A great part of this is a lower-class motivation, which would be found among all lower-class children. At many points, however, colored children mention the fact that even if they became educated, most skilled and professional fields would be closed to them on account of their color.

7. It should be strongly emphasized that nothing can be done to help the Negro child, in the sense of widespread social engineering, until his family has a chance to obtain a job, a living wage, a political voice, and an adequate education for its children. The problems of illegitimacy, delinquency, and desertion, which are tremendously more widespread in the Negro than in the white group, are certainly directly related to the economic and social disabilities of the Negro family (as a systematically subordinated group).

8. At the same time, there is urgent need for remedial work on personality lines with the great number of Negro children and adolescents who exhibit serious personality problems in connection with delinquency, illegitimacy, school work, and unemployment. In order to do such work effectively, child-study units should be set up for Negro children at selected universities. After a period of years, such units would be able to train remedial and personnel workers for Negro schools and institutions for delinquents. This seems the most scientific kind of remedial approach to the problems of illegitimacy, delinquency, and retardation.

To this summary, we may add several of the tentative conclusions of E. Franklin Frazier:

1. A large number of the children studied are assimilated

to the Negro world. The extent to which the fact of being colored affects their personality depends, then, upon the extent to which their isolation is broken down and the customary forms of accommodation disrupted. In other words, the effect of minority status is tied up with the development of self-consciousness. The Negro boy or girl in a lower-class family which has become accommodated to an inferior status is not likely to show conflicts, frustrations, and strains in his personality if he leaves school, say in the ninth or tenth grade, and accepts a job in a menial capacity. On the other hand, if a boy or girl from such a family develops an ambition to rise in the world, he may become conscious of the restrictions placed upon him because of race. Among upper-class children one may find conflicts and resentments growing out of the fact of race or he may find a complete identification with the Negro group.

2. The hopes and ambitions of many Negro youth and the roles which they expect to play are defined by the culture of the Negro world itself. This assimilation to the Negro world does not mean, however, that there is an altogether different set of values from those found in the white world. There is mainly a difference in emphasis or one might say that values in the white world are refracted through Negro culture. This undoubtedly affects the personality of the Negro youth.

3. The case studies show that the Negro has many of the same prejudices and outlooks that whites have. He even accepts what whites say concerning himself. In many cases he believes that Negroes are to blame for the way they are treated. Or he thinks that whites simply have the wrong idea about the race, that is, they judge the whole race by a few. Then, too, he shows considerable faith in the ability of the Negro to rise above his position. Upper-class children are very much inclined to place the blame on lower-class Negroes and to exhibit too much self-consciousness in their

effort to conform to white standards or to differentiate themselves from the Negro masses.

4. The low economic status of the masses of Negroes is of decisive importance in a study of this type. It forces Negroes to live in the worst sections of the community; it thereby isolates them from the whites spatially, economically, and socially. A large percentage of Negro youth grow up in broken homes where the mother is forced to work; they are exposed to all forms of vice and crime and therefore contribute a large percentage of the delinquency in the community. These facts determine the type of world in which the Negro lives.

5. When one studies in these cases the wishes and frustrations of Negro youth, they appear to be in terms of these limitations; lower-class youth wish above all for clothes and food and decent homes, whereas upper-class youth don't as a rule express a wish for these things but rather for money for conspicuous consumption and for personal achievement. In some cases it appears that lower-class youth attribute their disadvantaged position to the fact of color but this attitude did not show up as often as one might expect.

6. The response of the Negro to skin color cannot be considered in isolation; it must be considered along with the experience of the individual, along with his social position, his personal achievements, and so on. His attitude toward his own skin color grows out of the reactions of others to him. One may find good-looking, upper-class Negro girls of brown complexion desiring to have lighter skin, while on the other hand, one may find brown-skinned girls satisfied with their complexion. Where the girl expects to identify herself with an upper-class clique in which a light skin is highly valued, she will probably wish for a light skin. A dark-skinned girl who is identified with upper-class social groups and participates freely may have many inner conflicts which she would be unwilling to acknowledge. Lower-class, dark-skinned girls

may accept their dark skins just as they accept their lower-class position. Of course, it should be noted that the valuation placed upon a light skin represents a part of the Negro's assimilation in the larger white group.

7. The Negro group as a whole is very "healthy-minded" in regard to the fact of race. They seem to have a faith in the American dream. They seem to believe that money will help them to get ahead and help them to overcome the handicap of race, or that the fact of race will not make much difference.

After dealing with some of the questions above, W. Lloyd Warner stressed the following:

1. There is no such thing as a minority racial status to which all Negroes are oriented or have to adjust, but rather a hierarchical arrangement of individuals who share unequally in the goods, services, privileges, obligations, and burdens provided or imposed by the culture in which they live. In the higher strata a Negro physician may "interact" as much with whites as with Negroes: to some of both groups his class position may make him superordinate, and to others of both groups, he may be subordinate. In the lower levels, a Negro maid, for example, may be subordinate to her white employer, but superordinate to both whites and Negroes even lower than she in class status. Obviously, the "minority racial status" of the physician and that of the servant are quite different, and the way each conceives and feels about his "position as a Negro" is also distinct.

2. Among individuals of the same sex and social class, and even of the same occupation, if they share essentially the same "position as a Negro" in everyday social participation, they may differ in their conceptions of what it means and how it feels "to be a Negro" and this variation is frequently associated with variation in the circumstances of their early orientation. For example, to have been brought up in a situation where Negroes were strongly and consistently

subordinated by whites (as in some parts of the plantation South) is quite different from having been raised in a community where comparatively few Negroes were in much more intimate face-to-face relations with whites of analogous class positions and were even regarded as superior by whites lower in status (as in some sections of Chicago in 1910, and even in 1930). While it is probable that a Negro raised in the rural South would be clearly oriented to the caste organization of Negro-white relations as early as the age of 6, it is possible for one raised in Chicago to have been first oriented as "an American citizen—a person with full privileges in this society" only to begin to discover, at the age of 12 or 14, various forms of discrimination quite inconsistent with the "not castelike" definition of Negro-white relations to which he had first been conditioned.

3. One consequence of all this is that Negro individuals occupy a variety of positions, each having its characteristic patterns of personal adjustment. Negro youth, becoming adult in these various positions, experience a variety of definitions of their "status," which, especially as expressed in the schools, are frequently inconsistently interpreted for and by them in such a way that they may be exposed to severe conflicts in their basic identifications (as "a Negro along with all Negroes," "an American citizen," "just the same as white," "a person of light color along with others of light color," "not Negro, not white, but mulatto," and so on).

4. When a Negro boy or girl thus has his status defined in different and conflicting ways, anxiety over "being a Negro" may result, as has actually been observed in a number of cases examined. The individuals' attempts to resolve these conflicts may result in neuroses or more serious maladjustment, but generally preoccupation with such conflicts merely leads to somewhat obsessive and less efficient and less happy personalities.

Instead of stating the findings directly, Charles S. Johnson prepared a list of points based upon the entire research project which he thought represented points to be covered in any thorough discussion of the status of Negro youth. In fact, his outline could well be used by school classes and study groups as a guide to the analysis of the books in this series and other recent studies. First, Johnson gives general points and then those pertaining especially to Negro youth.

General factors to be considered

1. The objectively measurable factors of economic, educational, and health differentials which help to define the status of the Negro group in America
2. The aspects of the environment that Negroes can change, and aspects that they cannot themselves change
3. The changing pattern and character of the Negro family as a result of increasing acculturation
4. The accelerated development of social classes within the Negro population as a result of migration, education, and greater occupational differentiation, and the related emotional problems of status for Negro youth
5. The change from a fixed economic and social status in relation to the white population to a class pattern with less emphasis upon race and more upon class solidarity
6. The institutional character of race attitudes and the universality of this pattern which varies in intensity by areas as a result of difference in historical backgrounds, and the persistence of racial stereotypes and present economic tensions

Special factors affecting the adjustment of Negro youth

7. The problem of the communication of specific social, technical, ethical, and aesthetic standards and

values through the Negro family and community to Negro youth, and the relation of this to the fixed habits of behavior and inner controls of Negro youth

8. Delinquency and antisocial behavior as a phase of cultural and social maladjustment and misorientation
9. The limitation of occupational outlook and achievement by limited patterns of performance, and by dulled incentive
10. The role of color valuations in intraracial attitudes and relations
11. The dilemma of adjustment for personality stability to a cultural environment that is backward and obstructive to general racial development beyond a fixed racial status
12. The effect on Negro youth of the social implications of enforced racial segregation, both with respect to external groups compelling it and to the restricted cultural world in which they live
13. The protective covering and "avoidance" practices developed by Negro youth in response to their racial situation
14. Race attitudes toward whites, toward themselves as Negroes, and toward other Negroes as important in personality development

Then looking at his findings more from the point of view of what should be done next in a program of control, Charles S. Johnson concluded that:

1. In view of the lag of the large mass of the Negro population and consequent lack of development of new standards, emphasis in correction will have to be placed on children and the methods and content of their early education.

2. Corrective education should deliberately take into account their past racial role and development, with a view to its constructive change. It should aim further to provide substitutes for those features in the conventional procedure

which fail to take realistically into account the Negro youth's unique position in the American society.

3. For this group there is greater need for guidance clinics than, perhaps, for any other, because occupational opportunities as well as effective mobility are limited.

4. Other general recommendations might include specially devised parent education, delinquency clinics, apprenticeship opportunities, and provisions for the development of individual and group morale, as the larger problems of race and class find sounder solution.

THE SHADOW OF RACE

In concluding this summary we may observe that running through all of the area studies and through all of the lists of findings there was the persistent note that some of the effects of a castelike status are apparent in almost every Negro personality. In order not to overdo this point the investigators "leaned over backwards" to weigh all other factors that might condition a child's development. Some stressed the psychoanalytic approach to the point of studying all possible relations between such infancy experiences as weaning and later personality complexes. Others sought through family analysis to show how personality traits are formed. Others looked into economic conditions such as employment and housing for clues about Negro youth. In most cases all of these approaches and others were followed. The factor of minority status was studied as only one condition and in many cases it turned out as not the most important one. In spite of this insistent effort to see the whole picture and not overdo the conditioning effects of racial status, the shadow of race was ever present.

It enveloped some personalities more completely than others, but seldom did a Negro youth appear to escape to the clear atmosphere of a complete sense of freedom. White youth in America take so for granted their right to a place in the sun that they find it difficult to understand the almost inevitable defensive attitudes involved in being a Negro. When one is never sure when aspersions will be cast upon his group and upon him as a member of it, when one knows of certain limitations because of race but expects others most any time, when one can never escape his color even by convincing rationalizations but must live with a label which historically has been used to make people inferior—when these overtones are ever present, if not in one's immediate world at least in the background of his awareness, he can never be entirely free. He cannot be free in the traditional American sense that he can breathe deeply, square his shoulders, and walk down the street with no fears, no need for self-proof of his worth, and no need to overstress his achievements in some matters to compensate for lack of others. Psychologically, white freedom differs from colored freedom in America.

The disorganizing effects of this distorted type of freedom were found in every type and size of community, in every social class, in every occupational group. So subtle were its manifestations that some of the most "successful" Negroes denied its presence for they could not see its indirect effects upon their own personalities.

The self-attitudes reflecting the shadow of race varied widely. Some persons compensated through humor, others through extreme ambition, others through outright aggressiveness, and still others through reticence and withdrawal. But the presence of the shadow of race in some degree or in some form was the constant in the life experiences of all Negro youth. And as long as the dominent society continues to have stereotyped attitudes toward people of a certain hue, those who are of that hue will continue to rationalize, to conceal, or to shift attention to other matters, but they will never entirely escape psychologically their cultural heritage.

We turn now to the implications of all of the findings of

these studies with a concern that is commonly labeled "implementation." Or, more simply, we may ask: What can be done about it? Recognizing that ill-considered changes may create more conflicts than they solve, the recommendations which appear in the following chapters are stated tentatively as ideas that should be discussed, tried, and modified. A research study of these proportions should stimulate many persons and agencies to redouble their efforts and to try new approaches in the control of the problem. To persons and groups who seek an orderly improvement of this kind in the conditions which influence the personality development of Negro youth, the chapters in Part II are addressed.

PART II

CHANGES TO BE MADE

CHAPTER VIII

CHANGING THE STEREOTYPES

WALTER LIPPMANN gave the term "stereotype" a reputation and a popular usage in his now famous book *Public Opinion*. Involved in the following questions commonly asked about the Negro are many terms which Lippmann would no doubt call stereotyped ideas.

Why are they so shiftless and lazy?

. . . .

Why do they always have a chip on their shoulder ready to get mad and fight if anyone criticizes them?

. . . .

Why do they drop out of school so soon, not using to advantage the educational opportunities which they have?

. . . .

Why has not the race produced more great leaders?

. . . .

Why do they have more than their share of people on relief?

. . . .

Why do those who get a little money spend it all on cosmetics, clothes, and a car, instead of helping their less fortunate brothers?

WHAT ARE THE STEREOTYPES?

For years high schools and colleges have been trying to inculcate in their students the scientific spirit in the analysis of social problems. Nevertheless, when the question of race relations is up for discussion, few persons pause for the facts before drawing conclusions. The first step in an orderly control of the problem, therefore, consists in helping large numbers of people to recognize the common, often incorrect, and frequently inconsistent stereotyped notions by which the white world judges the colored and interprets the race question. Specific planning for Negro youth is futile so long as erroneous notions about them undermine intelligent support for programs of improvement.

"SHIFTLESS AND LAZY"
"ALL RIGHT IN THEIR PLACE"

Those who are glib in their judgments of "Negro character" are seldom troubled by inconsistencies in what they say. For example, many white persons are convinced that Negroes are by nature shiftless and lazy. Yet they commonly fear that these "shiftless and lazy" people may become ambitious to rise above their traditional role, or may gang together to stage some kind of minority uprising.

In the study of the rural South the interviewers found that if the Negro farmer prospered and built a good home for himself, he was often criticized by the white community. Several such farmers conccaled their modest wealth by not painting their houses or by not driving new automobiles. In the cities, the Negroes who live and dress well and have new cars are similarly criticized for trying to show off, but little is done about it. The white observer does not realize that the possibility of attaining such status symbols as a painted house, good clothes, and a streamlined car stimulate some Negroes to abandon the shiftlessness for which they had previously been criticized. If, as parvenus, they do not use their new possessions well, that is not an unheard-of fault among many peoples!

"NOT INTERESTED IN SCHOOLING"
"WHAT THEY HAVE IS GOOD ENOUGH FOR NEGROES"

In general Negro youth drop out of school early, and especially in rural districts many do poor work while they do attend. If the white critic who blames them for losing interest in school is sincere in wanting Negro youth to be better educated, he must be willing to help support an educational program that can accomplish this end.

The teacher may be the only representative of a better way of living with whom many children have intimate contact during their early years. If the schools are poorly equipped, the classrooms overcrowded, and the teachers underpaid, poorly prepared, and seldom promoted, there is little probability that the schools will provide youth with the needed stimulus.[1] If the white world remains content to provide an educational system that is "good enough for colored kids," it may expect to find succeeding generations of Negro youth "not interested in schooling," but efficiently educated in such things as poor work habits, racial animosity, immorality, and crime.

"HAPPY-GO-LUCKY AND CAREFREE"
"SULLEN AND RESENTFUL OF CRITICISM"

"You don't need to worry about mental hygiene for Negro youth. They are reared in a happy-go-lucky tradition and know how to drown their worries in song, laughter, religion, or corn liquor." As with many stereotyped generalizations about Negro personality, there is some truth in this flippant assertion. Most Negro youth are taught not to take problems too seriously because there is "nothing much we can do about them anyway." They soon learn that a good time is not planned for a year in advance but enjoyed at the moment. In an ecstatic religion some of them find an opportunity to transform their inferiority into an exalted status by joining God's chosen ones and contemplating the glories of the hereafter.

Taught to face life in these ways, many Negro youth never know that prolonged industry and postponement of personal

---

[1] For statistics on these conditions see Doxey A. Wilkerson, *Special Problems of Negro Education*, Advisory Committee on Education (Washington: U. S. Government Printing Office, 1939).

satisfactions are middle-class virtues which white people think they should have. They do not know what it is to plan for education, for marriage and family life, or to save systematically for old-age retirement. They consider themselves lucky if they have food for the day, money for a marriage license, and a midwife when their first child is born. They take life as it comes because that is the only way of taking it they know.

On the other hand, the white critic sometimes characterizes Negro youth in opposite terms as sullen, overly sensitive, difficult to handle. Some of them are. But the youth who is sensitive to insults and hardships is at least dissatisfied with present conditions. His discontent may be wasted in self-pity or resentment, but it may also be utilized and wisely guided.

Here, too, the white critic must make up his mind about Negro youth. If he wants them to be happy-go-lucky he should not criticize them for living in the present. If he wants them to become dissatisfied with themselves and strive for higher status, he must expect temporary maladjustment, be ready to guide the dissatisfied youth into a better way of living, and help to create conditions which will make it possible for them to improve.

WHENCE CAME THE STEREOTYPES?

There is little wonder that white persons prejudge and misconceive the nature of Negro youth. They learn during the first few grades in school about the Negro's status as a slave only two generations ago. They early learn from observation that in many relationships Negroes are still treated subserviently. The whole cultural atmosphere in which white youth are reared is conducive to the development of superiority and of patronizing attitudes toward Negroes. In other words, many of the stereotyped misconceptions are part and parcel of a culture of inequality. The castelike status of Negroes suggests to the "superior group" how their "inferiors" may be expected to act, and these prejudgments are seldom scrutinized or compared with the facts. They constitute a great handicap when Negro youth try to achieve self-respect and social status. Since it is difficult for white persons to sense how it feels to be so regarded, the psychology of caste attitudes might well be explained more fully.

HOW IT FEELS TO BE STEREOTYPED

Inevitably the dominant group in a caste relationship thinks of the lower group as not requiring or deserving conditions as favorable as their own. And, so long as Negro youth are not considered in terms of individual merit but categorically as on an inferior level, they are being deprived, first, of equal consideration before the law by the educational system and by industry, and second, of a full sense of personal pride and social recognition for individual achievement. Within their own group they may feel the urge to rise to higher levels, but when the general community continues to think of them as "just nigger kids," to segregate them economically to lower classes of work, and to insult them socially by ritualistic restrictions, the limits of their achievements are set and their discouragements multiplied.

"Oh, what's the use?" is the all-too-frequent expression of the Negro boy who might at one time have dreamed of becoming a construction engineer or a pilot on a commercial air line. Our culture has encouraged youth to have such dreams, but Negro youth have had to learn that they are not for them. Within the existing limits of opportunity, the achievement of individual Negroes has been remarkable and the elevation of group standards substantial in middle- and upper-class families. But, as pointed out repeatedly, with the great majority of colored youth born members of America's lowest third and with castelike restrictions helping to keep them there, one of the strongest motives—the desire for self-advancement and social approval—is available to them in limited measure.

Thus, caste and class barriers combine to the disadvantage of this minority group. And since the causes are dual, the solution must be also. As planning commissions are changing the externals of the Negro's environment by building him a playground or paving his streets, simultaneously the community must open the way to personal advancement for the individual himself. Freedom for wider job opportunities is the most urgent need, but the less tangible values of being thought well of, feeling at ease in the presence of other groups, and being "counted in" as an integral part of community life—these also are the things that men live by, regardless of the color of their skin.

PROBLEMS INVOLVED IN JUDGING BY MERIT INSTEAD OF BY STEREOTYPE

What would happen if Negro youth were judged according to individual merit instead of according to stereotyped attitudes dating back to slavery? Obviously, many members of the "superior group" would be fearful of their own positions. Many in the white community consider themselves the protectors of high family and community standards and therefore feel that they must keep at a "safe social distance" a group whose members they consider ignorant, shiftless, and immoral. Since these uncouth people are of dark skin they can be held "in their place" by an effective prejudice against all persons of Negroid appearance. So goes the argument. So goes the rationalization for categorical treatment.

But when the means for maintaining social distance between the groups is a purely physical trait like skin color, then many individuals of high education and refinement are excluded along with dark-skinned persons of low attainment. The total community is thus deprived of important contributions that some Negroes can make, and the individuals involved are deprived of community recognition. Possibly a national crisis will demonstrate the lack of wisdom of treating a whole sector of the population as a category set apart. If a labor shortage becomes acute in defense work, ability may be utilized wherever it is found.

But, on the other hand, if categorical discrimination is relaxed and the bars of segregation let down for Negroes of special merit, will not the lower masses also crowd in, taking advantage of the new freedom? This is the common fear of the white man. And, we repeat, fears on the part of every group must be taken into account in social planning.

The answer to this problem centers in the fact, often forgotten in race discussions, that white society itself faces identically the same situation. Just because all Caucasians are assumed to belong to the same general racial group and are not divided by caste barriers into separate compartments does not mean that all Caucasians belong to the same social groups. People associate in intimate groups, join clubs, attend dances and the opera, and most important of all select a mate in marriage on the basis of personal preference and common background. When the Negro asks for a chance to hold a good job, when he asks for the opportunity to educate his children and to occupy a decent house, he does not have in mind using this freedom to force his way into some intimate group of white people. And still more remote is the desire for intermarriage. Intermarriage is as taboo in Negro attitudes as it is in the attitudes of white persons. The voluntary associations of Negroes, as is true of all voluntary associations, are based on personal preference, mutual interest, and previous friendship.

White groups have too long engaged in parlor discussions of racial equality and intermarriage, and the bogeyman fears which have thus been engendered serve as a smoke screen obscuring the need for action on basic issues. Negroes are asking for good family and community life. They are asking not to be prejudged as a subservient group. They are asking to be included in the common life of the nation. Like all other groups, they want to enjoy the American way of life, and to help preserve and advance democracy according to their individual ability and where their contributions will count for most.

CONSISTENCY IN DEMOCRACY

These concerns constitute the real race problem to which the answer can be found only in the nation's basic moral attitudes. If our belief in democratic relationships, free competition, and recognition of personal worth is stronger than our tacit support of special privilege, unfair competition, and violation of individual rights, then our society will finally be willing to accept efficient Negro youth into economic and civic positions as it does other individuals of personal worth. The time has come for America to make up its mind as to what the basic tenets of its social organization are to be. Democratic principles and caste restrictions are antithetical. The American public should be encouraged to see that putting its own house in democratic order may well become one of its strongest defenses against totalitarianism.

WHAT IS TO BE DONE NEXT?

How can a people accustomed to judging a minority group as members of that group rather than as individuals learn to judge its members according to personal merit? How can our democracy solve within its own gates a relationship inconsistent with its declared principles? With the end in view of making people aware that dealing justly and adequately with the problems of race relationships is a fundamental part of making democracy functional, three recommendations are offered.

CHANGING ATTITUDES THROUGH PUBLIC DISCUSSION

Public discussion of our form of government and fundamental institutions is continually increasing; to further this discussion and to bring out its implications for Negro youth, the first recommendation is made.

All organizations interested in preserving and increasing the freedoms of democracy and all organizations concerned with the special question of race relations should take every opportunity to include "Negro Youth" among their topics for public discussion.

Many state and national organizations could assume special responsibility by including in their publications, as well as in their conferences, popular discussions of the place of minority groups in a democracy. This recommendation would apply to political parties, employers' associations, labor unions, the war veterans' organizations, federated womens' clubs, parents' groups, teachers' associations, denominational groups, youth agencies, chambers of commerce, service clubs—to mention only a few types. These state and national organizations might also provide lecturers and discussion leaders to assist local communities with their programs dealing with minority problems.

If the question of race relations is discussed within the broader framework of "freedoms and responsibilities in a democracy," many persons who had previously ignored it as an isolated and unimportant problem may begin to understand its relevancy to democratic well-being. Just as a professor of chemistry may have more effect than a minister upon the religious attitudes of a student, so a speaker or writer who mentions improved status for Negroes among the other democratic goals may have more influence than the agency which everyone knows is supporting the cause of the Negro. Into this broader realm of public discussion the question of race relations must move. Only as service clubs, women's organizations, church groups, youth agencies, educational conferences, professional societies, labor unions, and the hundreds of other types of voluntary groups in America begin to count in among their own concerns the way in which Negro youth have been counted out of the life of the community, can a change in point of view and practice be expected.

That progress in this direction can be made seems clear from the fact that it has been made in certain communities. In a small southern city when leading citizens and government officials began to discuss the problems of its Negro population as of concern to the whole community, specific projects in improvement were successfully carried out. In every state some community can be found in which little or great progress has been made, and citing such "success stories" may well be one factor in influencing public opinion in other communities.

CHANGING ATTITUDES THROUGH PRESENTING THE NEGRO IN A NEW ROLE

If the question of race relations is to be considered within the broader framework of the ways of democracy, then the Negro as a person must also be thought of in a broader reference. When white or mixed groups invite individual Negroes to appear before them, they generally ask the Negro visitors to follow one of four standard patterns: (1) sing folk spirituals, (2) play jazz music, (3) stage a superanimated dance contest, or (4) speak on the subject of race relations. In addition to these patterns Negroes should be invited to represent other interests. Toward this end the following recommendation is made.

Organized groups should invite Negro specialists to appear on their programs as a demonstration of the Negro's ability to succeed according to traditional American standards.

A Negro physical scientist or social scientist could be asked to discuss a technical problem in his special field. A Negro educator or writer could be invited to deal with a problem of general interest in educational methods. In these and other ways Negroes expertly trained could make their contributions as individuals.

The white community would come to think of Negroes more and more as persons, and less and less as representatives of a minority race or as objects of pity because of discrimination. The honorary degree conferred by the University of Rochester upon the scientist George Washington Carver as a part of its annual commencement exercises is an illustration in point. Another is the invitation extended by a southern medical society for a research doctor from Tuskegee Institute to address its annual meeting in Richmond, Virginia. James Weldon Johnson lectured at white universities on special fields of literature. Social scientists connected with this study of Negro youth have been invited by similar institutions to discuss, not "race relations," but theories of learning and personality development. These are ways in which the personal merit of Negroes can be discovered and recognized. As these ways are followed within different communities a new pattern in the recognition of merit among Negroes should gradually emerge and attitudes regarding the Negro become less rigidly categorical.

MORE BASIC METHODS OF CHANGING ATTITUDES

Although an informed discussion of the rights of minorities in a democracy or the appearance of leaders of a minority on programs of various kinds as accepted specialists may clarify the issues involved and lay the foundation for new attitudes, the realist in social change knows that such an approach, if taken alone, is too intellectualistic to be effective. Social change does involve a modification of attitudes; but, since social attitudes are generally acquired by unwitting processes and through emotional experience, "intellectualizing them away," though important, must be accompanied by other methods as well. Furthermore, a change in attitude does not necessarily bring a change in practice. When racial discrimination becomes as thoroughly entrenched and institutionalized as it is in the United States, change will come only as new procedures and patterns are substituted for the old. Therefore, another type of recommendation involving action as well as words is made.

Leaders in the various phases of economic and community life should introduce new patterns of race relations within the areas of their special influence.

This recommendation assumes that actual demonstration is one of the most effective techniques in changing attitudes and practices. In race relations, as elsewhere, the assertion that "it has always been this way and cannot be changed," is believed by many whose own liberal attitudes are ready for change but who are conservative about initiating new practices. When one can demonstrate not only that "it can be done" but that it has been done, fears are frequently relaxed and the new patterns gradually taken for granted.

Especially those patriotic, civic, and religious groups which by their very purpose are devoted to democratic idealism should be encouraged to apply their principles of social justice to racial barriers within their own organizations, and thereby set an example to other community agencies.

Similarly, private employers, labor unions, social agencies, medical and nursing associations, teacher associations, parent organizations, and other influential elements in community life should be encouraged to deal with racial barriers within their own groups. Just how fast the culture of any community can take such change must be considered in every case. Some would-be reformers have met disillusionment because the liberal pattern they sought to establish aroused such resistance from other members of their community that the net result was loss, not gain. On the other hand, waiting for all to agree that new patterns should be tried, means waiting forever in many communities. The rule is simple: attitudes and practices must change together, or one will conflict with the other. Putting the rule into practice is not so simple; it requires great insight, tact, and patience. In general, however, an appreciation of the processes of social change is more indispensable than a reformer's zeal.

To implement the three recommendations made in this section on "What Is to Be Done Next," either existing or new agencies should serve a clearinghouse function. In this way both private and public organizations interested in change could be supplied through publications, conferences, and advisory services with information about experiments in race relations that have already proved successful. The Commission on Interracial Cooperation has served this function to some extent. The National Urban League, the National Association for the Advancement of Colored People, the Department of Race Relations of the Federal Council of Churches of Christ in America, the National Commission on Ethnic Minorities of the YWCA, and other agencies have assembled and distributed information and are providing advice for groups interested in undertaking projects, but the work needs to be expanded greatly through either the present agencies or new organizations.

Certain types of communities have a special responsibility in modifying patterns of race relations, particularly in employment. They are the communities which have not undergone drastic industrial change in the last few years and which have a relatively small Negro population. Because industrial and social relationships in such communities are relatively stable, new patterns in this minor phase of their life can often be tried without danger. Once the pattern is operative here, other cities where change is more difficult to achieve would profit from the precedent.

Large-scale economic groups such as corporations and labor unions also have a special responsibility. Particularly in those industries where the workers are not in immediate contact with the customers, the corporation is relatively free to try out different types of labor policies. One of the largest automobile manufacturers has succeeded in introducing Negro workers in all branches of production and promotes them according to merit. This and similar examples help smaller employers who believe in such principles to initiate similar changes. No one is relieved from the responsibility of dealing with this problem, but certain communities and agencies should take significant leadership without delay.

THE UNIQUE ROLE OF GOVERNMENT

The largest employer today is not Sears, Roebuck and Company, A.T. and T., or General Motors, but the government itself. Unlike earlier periods in our history, today finds government the decisive factor in establishing many employment policies as well as other patterns of human relationship. All branches of government but particularly the federal hold a dual responsibility in race relations.

First of all, as the largest employer in the nation, government by its own personnel practices can determine the fate and welfare of thousands of Negro youth. Since federal appropriations call for uniform policies throughout the country, the federal government has a unique opportunity to provide Negro youth with hope such as they have never known. If both the federal government and those branches of local government subsidized by federal funds consider applicants not on the basis of race but of individual ability, Negro youth can see opportunity ahead where previously all doors have been closed.

In addition to the government's role as the largest employer, the federal and other units of government have an obligation to establish general precedents for fair dealing in all of their relationships with minority groups. Private agencies within the community will then be influenced to do likewise. Government units have a special responsibility to take such leadership because they are supported by taxation of all the people and thus represent all the people. Private groups may try to excuse themselves by referring to their limited purposes and exclusive membership. Government today is neither limited—it touches all phases of life—nor is it exclusive; all people pay for it and are governed by it. Every officeholder in a position of authority as far as establishing employment and other policies is concerned does not speak as a private citizen, does not speak as a representative of a special interest, but speaks in time of crisis and of peace as a preserver of democracy. His day-by-day decisions reflect his loyalty to that task.

The federal government, the governments of the forty-eight states, and even local governments have not been unmindful of this responsibility. Progress may be spotty and incomplete but it is not lacking.

Beginning with the President, incisive declarations of principle have been made. Nor has the matter stopped there. Executive orders indicating how these principles were to be carried out through the procedures of government have been stated with clarity and force. The following document is an example.

> WHEREAS it is the policy of the United States to encourage full participation in the national defense program by all citizens of the United States, regardless of race, creed, color, or national origin, in the firm belief that the democratic way of life within the Nation can be defended successfully only with the help and support of all groups within its borders; and
> WHEREAS there is evidence that available and needed workers have been barred from employment in industries engaged in

defense production solely because of considerations of race, creed, color, or national origin, to the detriment of workers' morale and of national unity:

Now, THEREFORE, by virtue of the authority vested in me by the Constitution and the statutes, and as a prerequisite to the successful conduct of our national defense production effort, I do hereby reaffirm the policy of the United States that there shall be no discrimination in the employment of workers in defense industries or government because of race, creed, color, or national origin, and I do hereby declare that it is the duty of employers and of labor organizations, in furtherance of said policy and of this order, to provide for the full and equitable participation of all workers in defense industries without discrimination because of race, creed, color, or national origin;

And it is hereby ordered as follows:

1. All departments and agencies of the Government of the United States concerned with vocational and training programs for defense production shall take special measures appropriate to assure that such programs are administered without discrimination because of race, creed, color, or national origin;

2. All contracting agencies of the Government of the United States shall include in all defense contracts hereafter negotiated by them a provision obligating the contractor not to discriminate against any worker because of race, creed, color, or national origin;

3. There is established in the Office of Production Management a Committee on Fair Employment Practice, which shall consist of a chairman and four other members to be appointed by the President. The chairman and members of the Committee shall serve as such without compensation but shall be entitled to actual and necessary transportation, subsistence and other expenses incidental to performance of their duties. The Committee shall receive and investigate complaints of discrimination in violation of the provisions of this order and shall take appropriate steps to redress grievances which it finds to be valid. The Committee shall also recommend to the several departments and agencies of the Government of the United States and to the President all measures which may be deemed by it necessary or proper to effectuate the provisions of this order.

FRANKLIN D. ROOSEVELT

The White House
June 25, 1941

Furthermore, separate government agencies have done

something about the status of Negroes within their own organizations. Certain agencies have been forthright and thoroughgoing in their efforts. They have invented new procedures to make employment more equitable and have even devised systems of voting on questions of government policy which have extended suffrage to all people concerned regardless of color. Other agencies have been lamentably negligent but everywhere the problem is "in the air." Government officials are considering to a greater extent than ever before how and when they must deal with it. Furthermore, many of them are not thinking of these improvements in the status of Negro workers as an expedient during a crisis but are taking precautions to see that the gains are permanent.

The specific measures taken by government in race relations are developing and changing so rapidly that what is true of the situation one day may not be true the next. This volume therefore states the principle that government as an employer and government as a leader in setting patterns has a unique responsibility. Other groups are not thereby relieved of their part, but rather the two types of social organization, private and public, must meet and solve the problems together. The role and responsibility of government is summarized in the following recommendations.

Every private organization, whether it be community, state, or national in its scope, should observe how government officials and agencies deal with race relations in their sphere of work. Those government agencies and officials who have introduced more equitable practices should be encouraged and their example followed in nongovernmental activities. Those who have not helped to develop more just methods of including all the people in their programs should be petitioned and in other ways urged to take the leadership which is expected.

CHAPTER IX

CHANGING LOWER-CLASS STANDARDS

A CHANGE IN the white world's conception of Negro youth is important if self-respect, pride, and ambition are to operate in their personality development, but even these objectives might be considered secondary, though not unrelated, to another need of Negro youth—a change in living standards.

THE DANGER OF LOW STANDARDS

This important and most sweeping problem is not directly concerned with the usual question of "race relations." As has been pointed out, the common discussions about social contacts and intermarriage between the races have touched off heated arguments, given rise to hysterical alarm, and obscured the urgent needs in the life of Negro youth which almost everyone would agree call for immediate action. The greatest "threat" of Negro youth to the standards of the general community is not that if given improved status they will "intrude promiscuously into its social circles" and will endanger the "purity of Caucasian blood." Rather, the threat of Negro youth to community standards lies in the fact that by and large they behave in a manner typical of a lower social class. As has been pointed out repeatedly, they do so because they are reared in the presence of substandard physical conditions and social incentives. The cost of Negro crime to the taxpayer and the property owner is tremendous. In many localities Negro delinquents and criminals are responsible for from two to six times as many crimes against property and violent crimes against persons as their numbers in the population would warrant. Racial crime statistics must be used cautiously, however, because of the greater susceptibility of the Negro to arrest and prosecution than is usually true of the white criminal. Even with this modification, it is still probable that the proportion of crime committed by Negro youth is high.

The Negro health hazard similarly undermines the welfare of the general community. With the death rate from syphilis five times as high among Negroes as whites and with high rates for tuberculosis and other contagious diseases, the health of all is endangered no matter how good the public health services are for the white population.

Negro housing is a related problem of general concern. Segregating the colored man to the deteriorated slums may keep Park Avenue socially intact, but it perpetuates alarming fire hazards and sources of disease in the congested living of the modern city. Similarly, in the rural sections the unsanitary and crowded conditions of Negro cabin life are an important factor in keeping the community's level of existence low. Finally, the social tastes, refinements, family life, educational interests, and general tone of culture cannot rise to high levels for the rest of the community if one-tenth are permitted to live on a permanently lower plane.

ESCAPING LOWER-CLASS STANDARDS

From the point of view of the community as well as that of Negro youth themselves, the solution calls for practical improvement in conditions of life. Greatly improved education, decent housing, economic security, opportunity for recreation, recognition, and community leadership—these are what Negro youth need urgently.

THEIR OWN BOOTSTRAPS

Although in the past many Negroes may have thought that their problems could only be solved through the help of the white man, there is now growing evidence that the Negro group can lift itself by its own bootstraps to some extent. Out of this new, though guarded, optimism comes the following recommendation.

Encouragement should first be given to organizations within the Negro group which are already striving for an improved status for their own race.

The Individual Approach

Self-improvement among Negroes has generally taken two forms. The first, an emphasis upon increasing the ability and status of the individual, has been prominent for many years in the programs of schools and churches. Booker T. Washington was the first racial leader to declare that if Negroes would become efficient workers they could go far in pulling themselves out of their state of misery. Since his time, many educational and religious leaders have preached a similar gospel.

In spite of Booker T. Washington's thesis, inefficient work habits and lack of skill are still altogether too prevalent. The explanation for this condition lies partly in the principle repeatedly mentioned to the effect that when there is little opportunity for advancement there is little incentive for improvement. For example, in one community a white home owner suggested that a colored yard man who makes a low hourly rate for cutting grass should receive a higher rate when he was given the opportunity to build a fence for the owner. Another resident replied, "No, you shouldn't spoil a good yard man. If you pay him more for carpentry he will be dissatisfied with his low rate for yard work. Just pay him the same and if you want to give him an extra fifty cents at the end of the job, all right."

When the typical American rewards for acquiring a new

skill and increased efficiency, namely, higher pay and a better job, are deprived Negro workers—and that is generally true in factories (where they are the janitors), on the farms (where they do the heavy, routine work), in the filling stations (where they grease the chassis but seldom manage the business)—then the white world cannot expect colored workers to become overly zealous about developing a high degree of proficiency. People are confirmed in good work habits by rewards. If the rewards are not forthcoming it is easy for a worker to become adjusted to a routine, hit-or-miss type of performance. The surprising fact is that so many colored workers have become proficient in the presence of such meager rewards.

This mixture of lower-class and lower-caste treatment of the Negro worker is not the only explanation for his not meeting more exacting standards of work. The schools, where vocational skills might have been taught, have received such low grants for work with their Negro pupils that except in rare instances neither adequate equipment nor trained teachers could be secured. If the white world criticizes Negroes for not being more efficient workers it is obligated to grant a more equitable share of tax funds for their training. The administrators of federal vocational acts have stated principles of equal treatment and have made a good beginning in carrying them out, but only as the drive for better training for Negroes gains still more momentum will its effects be felt where it is most needed—in the local communities.

There is still another explanation for lax work habits on the part of some Negro youth and this one is directly related to the topic of "lifting themselves by their bootstraps." Some of the Negro leaders have been so intent upon discussing the "race question" and criticizing the white world for its unfair and unequal treatment of the Negro worker that they have not exhorted the workers to do better with what they already have.[1] Some of the Negro colleges which do have vocational training are somewhat lax and complacent about their standards. The students are not always taught the immediate application of the skills they are learning to their own home and community. Some of the faculty members with secure income and professional status have not asked themselves disturbing questions about what changes their education is really making in the lives of their students.[2] After Negro educators and newspaper editors had condemned discriminatory practices in air corps recruiting they were somewhat embarrassed to find that at one of the centers where Negro applicants were invited to come for tests, no applicants presented themselves. It would seem that more effective work with their own youth group would have been in order at the same time that they were devoting attention to the question of discrimination.[3]

The National Association for the Advancement of Colored People was prompt in observing this need as is indicated by the editorial comment appearing in the May 1, 1941 issue of their *Bulletin:*

> The NAACP is much concerned about reports that full advantage is not being taken of vocational training courses offered

[1] Recognizing the importance of self-improvement and greater initiative among Negro workers, Ambrose Caliver, specialist in Negro education, U. S. Office of Education, commented on this section in the following terms: "I am particularly interested in your thesis concerning personal effort and efficiency. If anything, I would stress the point even more than you have. I have maintained for many years that whether the conclusion of this whole race situation in America shall be integration or separate independent economy, personal efficiency is essential, and the sooner we get away from attempting to hide our lack in this regard behind such phrases as group effort and cooperation (as important as these are), the better."

[2] This criticism could be leveled against hundreds of white educators but for the moment the subject is improving work habits and skills of Negroes, and consequently the point is stated in these terms.

[3] Another possible explanation is that Negro youth thought the announcement was too good to be true and only after their leaders assured them that there was no catch in the matter did they finally come to the recruiting centers. There is now an abundance of Negro applicants for every military and industrial defense opportunity open to them.

by the National Youth Administration and the Work Projects Administration.

There can be no justifiable basis for hue and cry about discrimination against our workers unless there are available men qualified to step into jobs when they are open. The reluctance of many men to spend time training for jobs in industries which bar them because of color is understandable, but so shortsighted an attitude will be fatal to the well-being of the race if allowed to persist.

The Group Approach

The second form which self-improvement among Negroes has taken stresses the importance of social movements and pressure groups which can secure from the larger community more opportunities and greater rights for members of the race. The National Association for the Advancement of Colored People has been such a militant group. Under the leadership of James Weldon Johnson, W. E. B. DuBois, and Walter White it has used court action, consumer boycotts, and appeals to public opinion in its attack upon many forms of injustice. A more recent organization, the National Negro Congress, also uses aggressive methods in its efforts to change social conditions. Working more in collaboration with white groups and supported to a large extent by white contributions, the National Urban League has tried to increase employment opportunities for Negroes, has dealt with problems of adjusting southern rural migrants to living conditions in northern cities, and has maintained a flexible organization so that new problems can be met as they arise. The Commission on Interracial Cooperation has made an outright attempt at cooperative undertakings involving both Negro and white citizens in many southern communities. It has been criticized by some of the more aggressive groups for what they consider its temporizing methods, but it has been praised by others who consider its approach realistic, not visionary, and its accomplishments substantial. Within separate communities many other groups have tried through political action, economic pressure, or appeals to liberal white persons to improve the lot of the Negro generally and, consequently, the status of the Negro individual.

The pressure groups have effected changes, but their work is complicated by the paradox that in so far as they succeed in arousing the masses to rebel against adverse social conditions they give the individual who is looking for a scapegoat an excuse for his personal failure. As pressure groups continue to announce how disadvantaged Negro youth are, some youth begin to believe that personal striving is futile. Thousands of white youth are faced with serious handicaps also, but they cannot rely on caste barriers as an excuse for personal failure.

This paradox need not concern us greatly. The inequalities are still so great that the need for social gains is imperative, even though a few individuals do not have the best possible attitude toward their own responsibilities. Nevertheless, while pressure groups are protesting against unfavorable conditions, they should try their best to do so in such a way as not to discourage the individual from self-improvement. Furthermore, in planning their strategy the leaders should avoid so far as possible those tactics which alienate the support of liberal white groups whose cooperation should be preserved.

To accomplish these ends, some agency might well invite leaders of all Negro reform groups to a special conference for the purpose of acquainting them with the findings of these and other Negro youth studies and of discussing with them the practical relationship between their programs of social change and the personality adjustment of Negro youth. An over-all policy-forming and service organization like the American Council on Education might well take the initiative in helping to relate research to action in this way. Or, if it is not possible for such a general educational agency to take the initiative, then one of the race relations groups like the National Urban League, the National Association for the Advancement of Colored People, or the Julius Rosenwald Fund could call such a conference. The specific purpose of the conference would be to re-examine the strategy of social change in the field of race relations. The effect of the reform movements upon the participants themselves could also be considered.

BOOTSTRAPS ARE NOT ENOUGH

Although Negro youth and their groups should be encouraged to face problems realistically, we must recognize that they alone cannot accomplish all that is desired. As already noted, the Maryland youth survey revealed that lower-class youth, regardless of their color, are so disadvantaged in their prospects for education and for a decent income that only outside forces can break the cycle. With the combination of class and caste handicaps, this is doubly true for Negro youth. The son of a white farm tenant may think it is futile for him to dream of becoming president, but any Negro knows that it is futile for him even to dream of becoming a commercial air pilot, and any Negro girl knows that a stenographer's job in a white business office generally is farther from the realm of possibilities for her than is Hollywood stardom for the white cosmetic clerk in the dime store.

Social planning in the United States has always given particular attention to the needs of lower-class groups. Strange it is, then, that planning conference after planning conference is called by both private and public agencies with only meager consideration given to that minority group which is affected by these problems in an extreme degree and in unique ways. This is true partly because the full facts about Negro youth have not been publicized, partly because trained specialists in Negro affairs have been unavailable, and largely because the white community has grown accustomed to seeing Negro youth reared on a lower social level. To help correct this situation the following recommendation is made.

All private and public welfare organizations—health, mental health, social, political, educational, occupational—which are dealing with youth problems should include on their planning staffs and in their service organizations trained persons who know the implications of these problems for Negro youth.

In order to acquaint such general welfare agencies with the facts about the Negro youth aspect of their problem and in order to arouse them to do something about these facts, a new type of working seminar, institute, or in-service training program is recommended. In the past there have been conferences on Negro health, employment, housing, and the like, but they have been relatively impotent because they were attended only by Negro leaders and a few casual white observers. This proposal is for a new type of study session devoted to Negro youth problems but largely attended by representatives of general planning agencies. The initiative in calling such conferences should be taken by agencies, private or governmental, which have not previously thought of race relations as their concern. This new and broader type of leadership is greatly needed if the habit of taking Negro youth's problems for granted is to be broken. The five collateral recommendations which follow will call attention to specific measures that might be taken in arousing social agencies of all types to discover the Negro aspect of their field of work.

Regional Negro youth conferences, institutes, or seminars should be held at convenient locations throughout the coun-

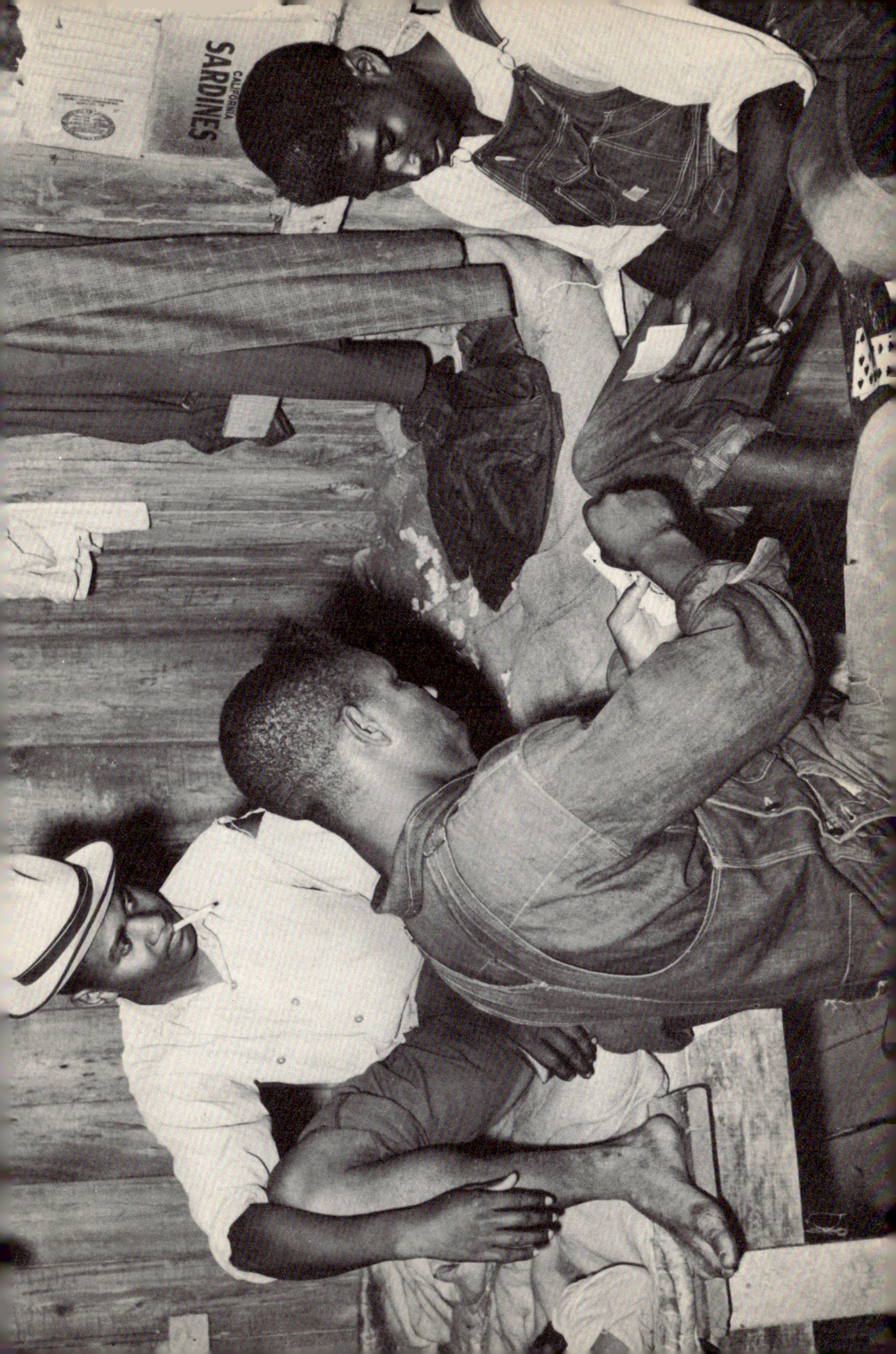

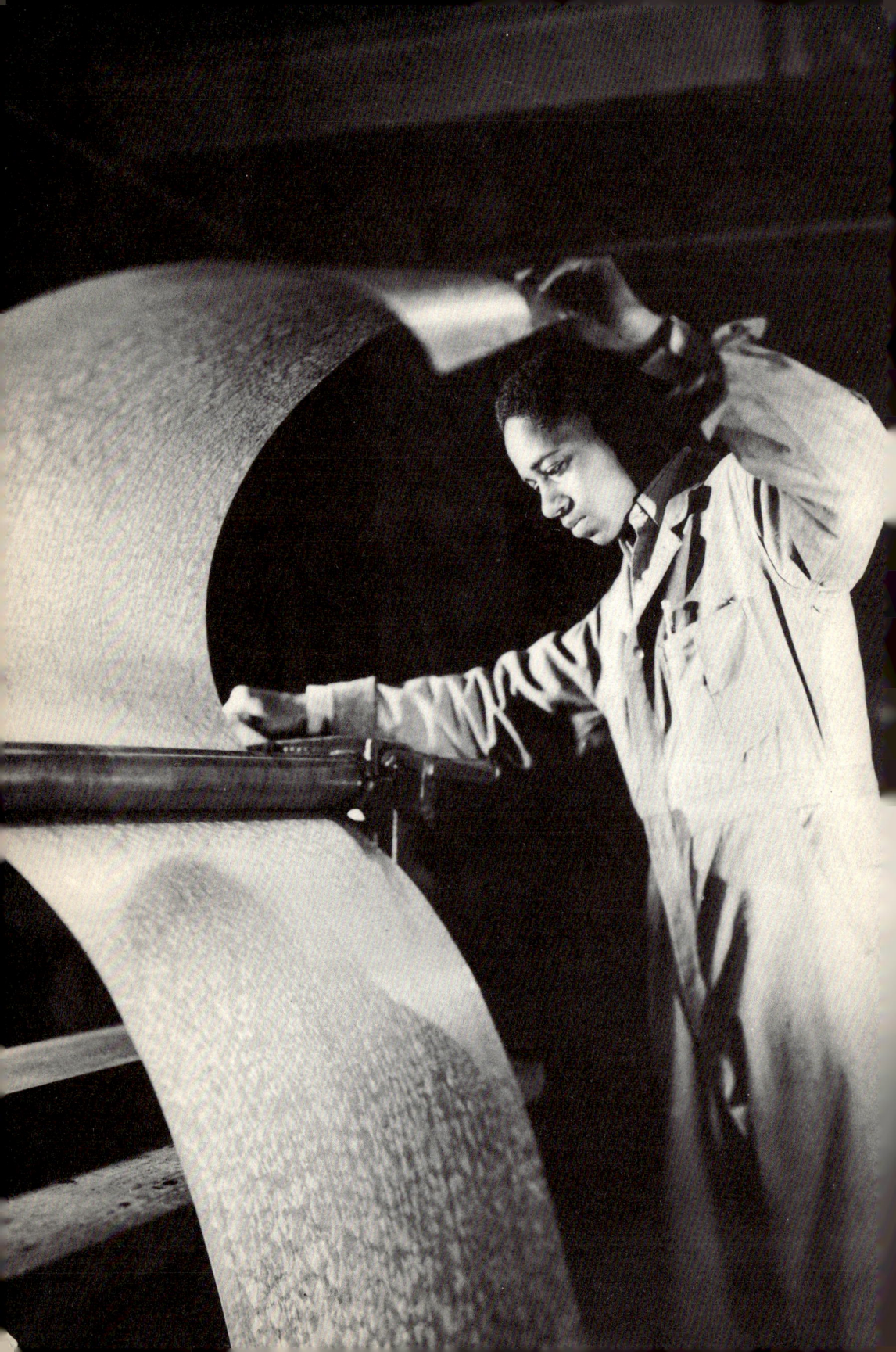

try as work sessions for representatives of all youth agencies and all types of social planning commissions.

The representatives of these general planning and welfare agencies should be invited (if necessary their expenses should be paid) to attend these meetings in which facts about the Negro youth aspect of their jobs would be graphically presented and frankly discussed. Such a project would be a worthy undertaking for foundations, clubs, federations, social work conferences, and other voluntary agencies, or for appropriate agencies of state and federal governments. Regional conferences of this type might be an especially appropriate project for Negro colleges or for institutions like the University of North Carolina, some departments of which have specialized in a study of Negro affairs, provided the cooperation of general community agencies were assured in advance.

Some of the Negro colleges have been necessarily preoccupied with meeting white academic standards. But now they must also see their unique opportunities for leadership in solving the problems of their own region. Within recent years many have awakened to these near-at-hand opportunities and could well sponsor such a project. A working institute or seminar carefully planned and attended by representatives of all types of youth agencies within the region should accomplish much in directing attention to the special needs of the Negro group and in developing methods that will be effective. Ten or twelve such seminars held in areas where the Negro population is concentrated should constitute an important step in improved conditions. Associations of colleges, social welfare organizations, or private foundations could take the leadership in bringing this about, and local colleges could assume the responsibility for the work session within a region. Relatively small financial outlays would be needed.

Specialized institutes dealing with particular questions of employment, housing, education, and health of Negro youth should be called to provide still more detailed information to those private and public leaders who are planning for certain needs of Negro youth.

A small appropriation from foundation funds would go far if leaders in community, state, and regional agencies were invited and their expenses paid to attend specialized work sessions concerned only with Negro youth problems. Once again it is emphasized that institutes on the health, employment, or housing of Negro youth if attended largely by Negroes are not enough. Some way must be found for establishing a new pattern of concern for Negro youth on the part of those who are in positions of authority in the welfare planning of the community as a whole. If a foundation of national standing would call, subsidize, or cosponsor such institutes they would be "respectable" and accepted, and agencies within the region would be inclined to cooperate. A change in conditions would not be assured by such institutes, but at least the initial step would have been taken. The next time a health, employment, or recreation agency started planning its work for the coming year it would be less easy for the staff to ignore the special needs of Negro youth. The representatives who had attended the institutes would have facts at hand about the Negro group and presumably would be interested in representing its special problems.

In-service training of a more thoroughgoing nature than the institutes or conferences just recommended should be provided for those staff members of private and public agencies who are responsible for work with Negro youth.

If necessary, scholarship funds should be provided so that concentrated study might be carried on during a leave of absence from employment. Certain social agencies have already established scholarships and leaves of absence for the further training of their workers. Specific training for work with Negro youth might well become a part of their program. With many community, state, or regional agencies, however, the workers could be released for special training in Negro problems only if voluntary organizations or foundations assisted financially through the establishment of scholarships.

It should be re-emphasized that this special study is not intended for the worker in an agency to whom the Negro cases have been assigned, but is intended rather for any worker, or better still agency supervisor, in order that he may have the opportunity to concentrate for a period of time on this aspect of his total job. Too many agencies have "handled" the Negro aspect of their program by merely appointing a special Negro worker. The greater need is for the entire agency to be aware of Negro youth needs when the program for the year is laid out.

Schools of social work, teacher training, and government service should recognize the critical problems of Negro youth by providing special courses of instruction as a part of the regular curriculum for all of their students, and advanced work should be given for those who wish to specialize in Negro youth work.

This should be one of the great pioneering fields in social, health, mental hygiene, and educational work of the next decade. In addition to offering formal courses of instruction, supervised field experience with Negro cases should be provided for social workers in training.

Popular ways of presenting facts about Negro youth should be devised.

Several motion pictures of the caliber of *One-Tenth of a*

Nation, The River, and *The Plow That Broke the Plains,* and additional radio broadcasts of the caliber of the series, "Freedom's People," should be produced to show the drama of Negro youth's struggle for an improved status. Such pictures revealing the different levels of Negro life and showing the effects of effort at improvement would be useful in schools, churches, and many types of adult groups. The production of the films could be sponsored by the numerous organizations which are now preparing and distributing educational films; only public insistence that this be done will bring to their attention this special need.

Small popular brochures giving factual data about Negro youth, such as *The Negro and Defense* issued by the Council for Democracy, should be prepared and distributed among all organizations that wish to give attention to the Negro question. Groups ranging from labor unions to missionary societies have their own publications (frequently including group study materials), in which the special needs of Negro youth are seldom presented. Now that so much material is available on the subject, editors should be encouraged to make popular summaries for their own members. Of special importance would be articles about Negro youth written for popular magazines. Since such magazines will seldom accept Negro material unless it is written by persons of prestige, special effort should be made to secure persons of national standing as authors of articles about Negro youth.

These suggestions are all based on the conclusion that the Negro cannot lift himself very far by his own bootstraps and that Negro youth constitute a special problem that will not be solved by a general "youth program." The Negro is a special problem partly because his conditions of living are unique, but also because the problems he shares with other youth strike him in such exaggerated form and have in the past been so frequently ignored. Any realistic effort at social control will require a more pointed program, better trained personnel, and a more enlightened public opinion than have existed in the past.

To make a start in this direction, the United States Office of Education has decided to sponsor five types of projects. Three of these are already under way and two are to be undertaken soon.

1. A series of dramatized radio programs and transcriptions on the participation of Negroes in American life. The major purpose of these programs will be to assist in the promotion of national unity in spirit and in fact.

2. An investigation of the courses and units of study on and about Negroes in schools and colleges in order to ascertain the number of institutions offering such courses and units and the nature of the work offered.

3. A leaflet on the contributions of Negroes to American culture to be included in the packet of materials for elementary schools being distributed by the newly created Information Exchange.

4. A series of pamphlets on education and the national defense, now in process of publication, including in appropriate sections discussions of the contributions of Negroes to American culture.

5. One volume of the *Survey of Higher Education of Negroes,* which this office is preparing, has to do with social and economic factors as they relate to the education of Negroes. Several sections of this volume treat race relations from an anthropological point of view and will probably have an influence in preparing the public for the more specific attack on the textbook situation by nongovernmental agencies.

CHAPTER X

CHANGING NEGRO EDUCATION, SOCIAL WORK, AND RELIGION

THE FUTILITY of "schoolin'" if it cannot be put to use; the priority of child labor over child education among many impoverished families; the antagonistic attitudes which unqualified teachers engender; the absence of individual attention when teacher load is high; the failure of the schools to solve many problems of social adjustment; the occasional case of parent-teacher-pupil cooperation in achieving good results under poor circumstances—these situations are all a part of the total picture of education for rural Negro children. And that means most Negro children.

> I ain't so worried 'bout my children getting all this schooling. They ain't going to do nothing nohow but work on the farm. I'll send them upon consideration up to the sixth grade, then they got to come out and help me. I went as high as the seventh, but it didn't do me no good. Unless you can go on to college, schooling ain't no 'count. My children just as well be home as chasing over there to that school house wastin' time and money.
>
> . . . .
>
> I like school. I always want to stay in school, but I reckon after this year I can't. Maw thinks I am big enough to stay home and work, and schooling costs so much. Sometimes I dream that when I am bigger I am going off and finish school, sometimes it seems like I am away at school.
>
> . . . .
>
> I would be further along in school than I am now, but when I was small I stayed in the Primer three years. I was just scared of my teacher. She used to call on me and I'd know my lesson, but she was so mean that when she'd call on me I'd get scared and couldn't say nothing. Then she'd whip me.
>
> . . . .

I've failed in the fifth grade twice. I reckon it was because the teacher was so very mean. She used to maul boys' heads with a big old ring she had on her finger. She used to say, "I ain't going to whip you hard, niggers, but I'll maul your heads with this ring I got on my finger." All the kids was afraid of her. It seems like every time she'd call on me my head would just go blank, I'd be so scared. I'm getting so I just hate to go to school.

. . . .

I don't know what is the matter with that blockhead. Me and his mother done everything for him, but he just won't do no good. He ain't been near no school for three years and he's 17 now. I just wish I had the opportunity he had when I was coming along. The world expects more of him than it does of people like me. I'm going down and he's coming up, but he won't go to school.

. . . .

I might could do better if Miss James woulda showed me how to work those fractions, but she would just pass me on by and let them that understood it work the problems all the time. She'd say she didn't have time to be bothered with trying to help all of us dumb ones who just didn't understand. She said we just oughta study more, but I know I studied all I could.

. . . .

I believe education is like this: If it prepares you to do something, then it's all right. Now, I believe a person ought to go as far as the eighth grade. After that he ought to take a trade—bricklayin' or plasterin' or something he can work at with his hands. All those people you see 'round Clarksdale and in the city what done finished up, walkin' 'round holdin' their hands, with nothing to do.

. . . .

Every year when school opens I goes down to the school and see his new teacher. I tell her what I want my son to learn and how I want him to act. My boy is a good student; he gets his lesson fine. If something goes wrong at school I goes down and see what the trouble is.

As long as it is possible that a Negro college graduate trained in elementary education is forced to give up her position as a schoolteacher and take a job as a maid at $10.00 a week in order to increase her annual income, standards of education will continue to be dismally low. Low standards of pay and personnel in the Negro schools help explain some of the problems reflected in the quotations taken from Charles E. Johnson's southern rural study.

Ira DeA. Reid's *In a Minor Key,* Charles S. Johnson's *Growing Up in the Black Belt,* and Doxey A. Wilkerson's *Special Problems of Negro Education*[1] are well-documented studies of the unequal distribution of school funds for Negro children. These studies prove and dramatize the need for equalization of finance within states and local districts as between racial groups and also within the country as a whole as between areas of varying wealth. The tax base throughout the country varies so widely that only through the supplementary use of federal funds can standards of public education be raised for all the people.

The purpose of this chapter, however, is not to reiterate these compelling facts about inequality nor to praise the institutions for their educational accomplishments against odds, but rather to show how the teachers and social and religious workers can accomplish still more with what they have, as well as to point out what they can accomplish when they do get the much needed better schools and salaries. This chapter deals also with the frame of mind of the teacher, the social worker, and the religious worker and the way they regard the youth with whom they work. The field research has something practical to say about these intangibles.

TEACHER-CHILD RELATIONSHIPS

Teaching and social work are predominantly middle-class occupations. The salaries paid for such work, especially in rural districts, are low. The social status is relatively high, but generally not at the top, at least not at the top in the largest communities where a few Negro doctors, lawyers,

[1] Advisory Committee on Education (Washington: U. S. Government Printing Office, 1939).

and government officials acquire still higher status symbols. Since the majority of such workers are better off than the lower classes, but not socially eligible or rich enough for the upper, they are on the move socially and are often very conscious of this fact. Furthermore, those who manage the schools and social agencies also have a middle-class bias and judge the success of the teachers and workers by the number of youth they can prepare for "respectable" middle-class living. One teacher in Louisville was so conscious of the status factor in her own social adjustment that during a conversation with an out-of-town visitor she concealed the real facts about the number of her pupils who were receiving free milk at recess time, lest the visitor identify her with a slum school and slum area.

Because of their own social adjustment problem, many teachers are biased in favor of those pupils who are already clean, obedient, subdued, and diligent in their studies. They are the model pupils who make the teacher feel that he is a success. It is not surprising if he gives to such pupils special favors, responsibilities, and recognition. The teacher can readily tell which children come from parents who reinforce the patterns of the classroom in their out-of-school relations. He knows that such parents are "on the side of the teacher," making his task easier by inculcating in the children an expectation of school success and an awareness that education is a prerequisite to later achievements. The teacher also knows that these parents are members of the community's middle or upper class, and he wishes to remain in their good graces, or possibly to win their approval.

If by chance a lower-class mother should come to the principal's office to inquire about her son's standing at the same time as an upper-class mother, the principal would not only recognize the difference in their status by their dress and manner, but would also find it difficult not to show greater concern for the adjustment problems of the son of the upper-class parent. It would not necessarily be for the crude reason that he was trying to curry favor, but rather because he and the upper-class parent have a common outlook. The result is, nevertheless, that privilege begets privilege in subtle ways.

The general preference of teachers to work with the more cooperative pupils and associate with the "better class of parents" is reflected in their not infrequent requests to be transferred out of a "poor school," meaning out of a district of lower-class children, when transfers or promotions are made. True, some are willing to remain where they think the need is greatest but they do so in spite of class training not because of it.

All of this is also true of schools for white children; their teachers and principals are generally upward-striving, middle- or upper-class people. Even so, Negro schoolteachers sometimes outdo their white colleagues. Because they cannot escape a low *caste* status, they have stronger reason to enhance their status in the *class* structure. Furthermore, teaching is one of the few types of employment which will enable Negro women to rise socially. Small wonder then that some colored teachers are especially out of sympathy with "uncooperative pupils" and especially favorable to children whose middle- or upper-class background makes their school conduct more in keeping with the teacher's own way of thinking.

In recent years, teacher training institutions have tried to alter the situation. When they have emphasized the needs of the child and especially of the underprivileged child, the result has often been the development of a sympathetic attitude in teachers without their acquiring an understanding of the socio-psychological forces involved in the personality problems of children. Neither a sentimental regard for the child nor an impersonal testing program is a substitute for a full comprehension of the factors involved in each case.

Only such understanding will enable the teacher to provide substitute incentives which will permit the child to succeed in new patterns of conduct.

Visiting teachers, psychiatric social workers, child guidance clinics, improved economic conditions, and many other things are needed, but the teacher himself has a responsibility and an opportunity. His attitude toward children whom other persons have misunderstood, his realization of when to give encouragement and in what form will make him a determining influence of great importance in the lives of many children who are vacillating between one cultural world and another.

AND WHAT OF THE SOCIAL WORKER?

Trained social workers might be expected to have more insight than school teachers about the Negro youth with whom they deal because they have been taught more about human nature as part of their preparation. Furthermore, while they also have a middle-class bias, it is apt to do less harm because social work training has always stressed a sympathetic understanding of lower-class conduct.

Unfortunately, these assumptions are unsupported by facts. Of all Negro youth, only an occasional one ever comes into contact with a professionally trained social worker. In many communities private social agencies do not welcome, and certainly do not solicit, colored clients. Public agencies generally receive them, but in many such organizations the worker is a dispenser of relief or a determiner of eligibility— and not a sympathetic counselor with the time, patience, and training to give lower-class Negro youth the encouragement and continued counsel they need. An exception to this rule may be found in an organization like the Institute of Juvenile Research in Chicago or the Family Society in Philadelphia, whose staff members could pull from their files numerous records of thoroughgoing case work with Negroes.

But, for Negro youth as a whole, social work is as unable as education to claim credit for saving them from an endless chain of lower-class influences.

ORGANIZED RELIGION

Because the ministry has been one of the few professions open to Negroes with ideals for service and with status aspirations many have responded to the call to preach. The better established churches and denominations with membership drawn primarily from the middle and upper classes have developed high educational requirements for their ministers. But the pentecostal sects and the more informal denominations which serve the lower classes have accepted those who have the will to preach without setting educational hurdles in their way. The result has been that only in the field of religion do Negroes have leadership proportionate to population. In medicine, nursing, law, teaching, and all other white-collar work there are fewer Negroes per thousand persons than in the white population. Proportionately, however, there are more ministers for Negroes than for whites.

As a consequence there are many Negro churches. The pentecostal groups and many of the largest congregations among the old-line denominations welcome all who wish to come. Regardless of his class position any Negro who has not openly violated important moral sanctions can find a group which will give him support and encouragement. Even if the gospel of some of the churches is otherworldly, the welcome into the group is cordial and helps the low class and the outcast of this world to have a sense of "belonging."

A survey of organized religion among Negroes reveals, however, that from the standpoint of social class characteristics, differentiation is by no means entirely absent. There is as wide a range in type among colored as among white churches. The emotionalism of the pentecostal sects and the offer of salvation to all sinners who repent is almost identical with the behavior of some white churches today and of many white groups in camp meeting days when they did not feel compelled to stress education, restraint, and social respectability. At the other extreme are Negro churches (some indeed belonging to so-called "white denominations") which have an order of service, an educated ministry, and a trained church school staff which resembles that of a white church in an upper-class suburb. Among these are some Negro institutions which are carrying on an intelligent program of education for their own membership as well as for the less fortunate in their community, though the latter program is on a mission or settlement house basis. During the northward migration following the last war certain of these churches in the industrial cities were more responsive than other community agencies to the needs of migrant families who were ill-adjusted to their new environment.

Much has been said in the past about the church as the center for the social life of the Negro group, but times are changing in Negro religion as well as in white. Churches are tending to become highly specialized institutions with a few scheduled meetings. The social function of the Negro churches is still present in varying degrees, however, and in some of the more "progressive" churches is being re-emphasized.

Religion for Negroes is not entirely their own affair. Long before emancipation and ever since, the "uplift" of colored people has been a prominent objective in the program of many white religious groups. Although working with the Negro community used to mean social ostracism for the white missionary, denominations continued to send preachers, doctors, and nurses. Today, such predominantly white groups as the Federal Council of Churches of Christ in America, the YMCA and YWCA, and certain church denominations have a special phase of their national program devoted to improving religious work among Negroes, developing more harmonious race relations, and bettering the status of the Negro population generally. The "Race Relations Sunday" is an example of a new pattern which has been developed to bring the religious groups of the two races more closely together in their understanding of each other's problems and aspirations.

Counteracting these favorable reports, the critics of organized religion point out that many churches professing brotherly love discriminate as quickly against the Negro in their own meetings and annual conferences as do secular agencies, that within the better organized Negro churches class lines are subtly drawn in such a way as to make the person of low status feel unwanted, and that the leadership of many of the Negro churches emphasizes formal theology instead of giving friendly aid to persons who are really in need of social support. Certainly many of those who are being trained for religious work with Negro youth are in need of new insight about personality adjustment just as schoolteachers and social workers are. We shall turn now to the question of just how these three professional groups should regard their special responsibility with reference to Negro youth.

SPECIAL PROBLEMS OF NEGRO YOUTH WORK

Education, social work, and organized religion should regard Negro youth as a special responsibility for two reasons. The first concerns the fact that Negro youth are so handicapped by other aspects of their environment that only as these agencies come to the rescue can a change in the cycle of retarding influences be expected. The cycle is this: Many Negro youth are born into families and neighborhoods lacking in compulsions and cultural rewards that make for ambitious, disciplined living. These youth accustomed to taking life in a rough and ready way bring their children into a world of influences similar to that of their own childhood. Complacency begets complacency.

The cycle continues generation after generation unless broken. Just as special educational and health measures were needed (nurses on horseback, and settlement schools which go to the people) to combat degenerate living in the backwoods country of several of our states, so special methods must be developed to reach the majority of Negro youth whose environment is impoverished in socio-psychological incentives. Schools, social agencies, and churches are society's best means of breaking the cycle, but in the past their methods have largely been borrowed from another setting and have been too stereotyped.

The second reason why these agencies have a special responsibility is that they are in a position to deal with personality problems of Negro youth whose outlook has been distorted by interracial or other experiences. The sullen youth, the resentful one, the fault-finder, the suspicious one, the one with a quick temper, the one with little ambition, and others whose personality type is a bit off center may not have been made that way by racial experiences, but as we have seen in earlier chapters they often express these traits in racial terms. Schools, social agencies, and churches should see a special responsibility for re-educating by changing the attitudes and emotions of the minority group. If they do not make Negro youth more objective about their world, do not give them more insight about what methods will succeed and what will get them into still more trouble in interracial relations, and do not teach them traits and attitudes which in the long run will bring better personal adjustment and group progress, then they will continue to miss a special opportunity. These agencies have too often dealt with Negro youth as though they faced no special problems. Realism should replace wishful thinking if the problems are ever to be reduced and eventually eliminated.

INADEQUATE TRAINING OF PERSONNEL

In order to overcome their deficiencies, the schools, the churches, and the social agencies should have specially trained personnel, the best equipment, and the most progressive methods of work, but the reverse is more likely to be true. For example, with few exceptions, both white and colored teachers of Negro children have been prepared in traditional teacher training institutions in which curriculum, goals, and methods were based on middle-class white standards.

A white teacher in one of the small northern communities included in this study, having completed her training course in the sedate atmosphere of her home-town college, was assigned to one of the "better schools" for her practice teaching. After a year's unemployment, the only permanent position she was offered was in a "Negro and Mexican school on the south side of town." She soon found that the classroom methods she had previously used did not function. Without trying to analyze the problem further, she accepted the dictum of her colleagues on the staff that "You can't be nice to these kids. You've got to lay down the law and let them know from the start who is boss." After having adopted the prescribed "hard-boiled" methods, she reported, "I'm a nervous wreck every night when I come home from school, and I don't feel I have accomplished a thing."

Thousands of miles away, a colored teacher in a rural Negro school faced a similar predicament and her "solution" was the same. Although she had studied child psychology in one of the large city colleges, she depended heavily upon a hickory paddle as a teaching aid in the classroom. She was not concerned about the family background and the future

vocations of her pupils; if she could keep erasers from flying while she completed the routine of assignments and recitations for six hours a day, she was satisfied. And if, during the early spring, the "worst boys" dropped out of school to plant cotton, she considered herself doubly blessed.

EXCEPTIONS TO THE RULE

Some teachers and social and religious workers, through a fortuitous combination of superior training and unusual personality traits, bring to children real insight and sympathy. By sensing the strategic moment when a child of lower-class background can be given approval for a step taken toward a higher standard, the adult becomes a social force of momentous importance. And, if in addition to his own efforts, the worker can skillfully encourage groups and individuals with prestige in the community to include the new recruit for middle-class respectability as though he already belonged, he has gone far in overcoming the child's loyalty to a lower-class culture which was previously his source of social approval. A number of "success stories" could be cited of teachers and social and religious workers who put the social needs of the children ahead of their own status, and who had the insight and skill to make their good intentions effective.

The ease with which such an approach can influence the personality development of Negro youth was accidentally demonstrated in the course of this study when the friendly interest of a middle-class interviewer gave a child who had slipped to lower-class status a new sense of confidence. Her deportment rose from "problem child" to "perfect," and her grades from failures to superior marks. These were objective evidences that inner changes had taken place. The establishment of close rapport with the child through many interviews revealed to the research worker the nature of the change.

The process was a simple one. The child discovered in the interviewer a friend from a higher social world who had confidence in her ability to rise. The interviewer was not shocked by the child's inferior home conditions, she was not shocked by the moral breakdown of the child's family, she was not even shocked by her poor deportment and low academic standing in school. Unlike some preachers or teachers who would make the child feel so guilty because of these conditions that she would be forced into some form of compensatory behavior, the interviewer took the child as she was. She gave her friendship which was what she needed most of all. She gave her approval for the struggle she had made although her success had not been great. And this, the child needed rather than criticism. Then she gave encouragement—a new kind of encouragement. She did more than pat the child on the shoulder and admonish her to become an "A" student. Rather she patiently helped the child think through all of her plans—see frankly what stone walls she was up against, see what efforts would be most likely to succeed, and encouraged her to take the first steps in this direction.

Furthermore, the interviewer did something constructive toward improving the child's environment. By explaining the situation to the teacher and to the parent, she made the child's world more friendly toward her. Had the interviewer gone further by enlisting the help of two or three secure adults in the community who could have continued to give encouragement and support the social therapy would have been complete.

Achievements of this type have been rare in the past principally because teachers and other youth workers have lacked the insight which a thorough knowledge of the social class and caste system would bring and because they themselves have been so involved in the struggle for status that they were blinded to the opportunities of achieving for their pupils what they had sought for themselves. There is unfortunately one additional reason why this type of helpful understanding is rare. The teaching and case loads have been so large that individual analysis and therapy have had to give way to mass treatment.

For a number of years educators have talked as though they had discovered that the development of the individual child is their basic interest. Nevertheless a high proportion of Negro children have not yet been touched by progressive theories of instruction and this is particularly true in the elementary schools of the rural South where most of Negro education takes place. Furthermore, the most progressive schools in the cities, which are organized to take account of individual differences in their pupils, have not begun to educate their teachers in an understanding of the social compulsions of class and caste factors which lie behind many differences in behavior.

A PROJECT TO IMPROVE NEGRO EDUCATION, SOCIAL WORK, AND RELIGION

If these middle-class outsiders, who in the past might have broken the chain, have often missed their opportunity, the following recommendation for the future becomes increasingly urgent.

A foundation, a state department of education, a state school for Negro education, a private college for Negro education, a group of social agencies, or a combination of these agencies should establish a new type of guidance center for Negro youth in which the complete personality development and adjustment of the individual is the center of interest.

Before this recommendation is considered further its objectives should be clearly stated. The first objective would be to test in practice the theories of how the personality development of Negro youth may be improved which this study of Negro youth and other recent research studies have postulated.[2] The second objective would be to provide demonstration centers in which representative educational, social, and religious leaders could receive training in a new type of guidance work through actual participation in the projects.[3] The third objective would be to develop techniques and procedures which could be communicated to larger numbers of workers engaged in educational and youth-serving organizations.

In setting up such centers, the following points should be considered.

1. The selection and training of the staff for these centers would be of paramount importance. The members should be persons capable of combining the cultural and psychological approaches to personality analysis. They should be given an extensive training program involving the use of the research materials of this and other studies before starting the work of the demonstration project.

2. The youth selected for participation in the demonstrations should represent different social levels.

[2] This project is based on the assumption that if youth workers study the "expected behavior" of Negro youth as revealed by the area reports, their insight for dealing with cases in their own agencies would be greatly increased. Such descriptions of expected behavior should be very useful in helping workers understand the source of personal conflict, feelings of inferiority, lack of ambition, lack of response to higher standards, and so on. The social worker, for example, can then study in a particular case whether or not the individual accepts the restrictions placed upon him, withdraws from the realities of the case, seeks substitute gratifications, or resorts to segmental satisfactions in a pathological way.

[3] When T. Arnold Hill studied the details of this project, he added that its effects should also be felt in labor union practices where the Negro workers have suffered discrimination and that leaders in industry and government should be included as well. He stated: "I believe further the plan should provide for the use of labor leaders or potential labor leaders, as well as teachers and social workers; and I should hope that, in recognizing as you do the importance of the economic and employment phases of Negro life, we might find occasion to utilize industry and governmental offices to further the training of staff members. I feel also that the plan should carry some provision for a period of 'internship' in or exposure to employment offices and personnel divisions of industry, and perhaps business offices of labor unions and any places where contact with jobs is usually made."

3. After the demonstrations are in progress, a group of teachers and social and religious workers should be invited to affiliate themselves with the projects in such a way that they could observe and participate in the new methods of instruction and guidance.

4. Carefully selected members of the staffs should participate in teachers' institutes and other training programs in an effort to carry their findings to a broader field. Several staff members should spend a part of their time as field consultants traveling from school to school, holding conferences with administrators and teachers in their own situations for the purpose of bringing about a deeper understanding of and a new approach to the personality adjustment of Negro youth.

5. Other members of the staff should be lent to educational workshops, to publication projects, and to any other undertakings that would bring to prospective or experienced teachers and social workers a realization of the need for a new type of skill in meeting the problems of Negro youth.

6. Recognizing that nonprofessional people may also influence youth other staff members should serve as consultants in parent education and other types of adult education so that middle- and upper-class citizens of the community may bring to disadvantaged Negro youth incentives and encouragement for educational and social attainment.

In short, these demonstration centers should develop effective methods for reaching a class of Negro youth who today are largely immune to the influence of both schools and social agencies. Having learned how to make the new incentives effective, the centers would then teach the insight and skill to others both through work at the center and through field service.

For the sake of concreteness, the implications of the field studies have at this point been stated in the form of a demonstration guidance project. It should be understood, of course, that no teacher or youth worker, no school, social agency, or church need wait for the establishment of elaborate experiments. With the principles well in mind, many persons should be able at once to take beginning steps in the improvement of the work of the schools and social agencies in the personality development of Negro youth.

The Jeanes teachers, supported by the Anna T. Jeanes Fund, have for a number of years made an excellent approach to the educational needs of southern rural Negro youth. Their approach is to work directly with and through the rural schools in such a way as to come close to the lives of the people. They are as proud of their achievement when the families in their county become ambitious for screens on the windows of their cabins as when a modern textbook is adopted. Each summer the Jeanes teachers attend a training institute where they can share experiences and acquire new techniques. The Julius Rosenwald Fund has worked for the improvement of Negro education in the rural South by helping to provide better school buildings and a better trained personnel when local authorities are willing to do their part.

Since the fall of 1939 two Negro institutions have been associated with the cooperative study of teacher education sponsored by the Commission on Teacher Education of the American Council on Education. Representatives of these institutions have participated in all general meetings, conferences, and workshops held in connection with this study. Furthermore, several of the public school systems associated with the cooperative study which have large numbers of Negroes in their constituencies have been particularly alert to the needs of their Negro teachers and sent them to workshops and other types of conferences and meetings. Fellowships have also been granted to many Negroes from institutions associated with the Commission program, particularly for study in the field of child growth and development.

Some of the state departments of education are all too willing to condone inequality in schooling for Negroes, but in other instances the personnel of these departments have taken seriously their responsibility for improving the conditions of Negro community life as well as education.[4] The project now to be described was conceived by such a state official. Much more should be undertaken, however, by other agencies both in the rural South and in all communities where Negro youth live.

Through the assistance of the General Education Board and the Texas State Department of Education, Prairie View State Normal and Industrial College in Texas started a novel project during the summer of 1941. In most educational workshops teachers predominate. At Prairie View the fifty persons who came together for three weeks of study included farmers and their wives, teachers, school supervisors, and business and professional people. The group consisted of ten representatives from each of five different communities. A cross section of each community was secured so that new ideas about living and schooling would have a better chance of being incorporated in the life of the community than if only the teachers had come.

Several truck loads of home and school furniture that needed refinishing and machines that needed repairing came with these people. The members of the "class" were taught how to improve their way of living by practical demonstrations of how their own beds and mattresses could be repaired, how the schoolrooms could be made more attractive, how the farmer's dollar could be made to go farther, and how the soil could be made to produce more.

At the same time that this novel type of workshop was in progress, another group was studying more pointedly

---

[4] Ambrose Caliver, *Supervision of the Education of Negroes as a Function of State Departments of Education* (Washington: U. S. Office of Education, Bulletin 1940, No. 6).

the human nature of Negro youth living in those communities. Under the leadership of a mental hygienist who had previously visited their communities, twenty teachers of elementary and high school youth studied the materials in the American Youth Commission publications. The new insights about personality, class and caste influences, group therapy for distorted attitudes in the individual, and other human phases of the job of teaching were discussed in relation to the communities and schools from which the teachers had come. The instructor held individual and small group conferences with members of the class in an effort to help them plan new approaches to the adjustment of Negro youth in their own schools.

The same instructor conducted a similar course at Texas College during the summer of 1941 and had the satisfaction of seeing members of the class turn theory into practice by trying to use incentives which would stimulate families in the community to improve their standards of living. Several case studies are available in which tangible results were secured in only one summer's work.

All of these projects are a partial beginning. They need to be more thoroughgoing, still more closely related to the place and ways youth really live, less academic in method, and more a part of the group processes already at work in the school and community. Although more could be hoped for, they do illustrate that teachers as well as adults with little formal schooling can acquire a new understanding of the factors that are shaping the lives of youth, and can do something about it. The demonstration projects recommended are designed to speed this process by becoming training centers where teachers, social workers, and community leaders can observe the way personality traits are acquired and modified.

Such a method of instruction is used in nursery school education and in teacher training demonstration schools, but the few such centers available to Negro teachers are organized to illustrate general aspects of the learning process and are not related to the historical background of Negro youth, to the variations in class position of the families from which the youth come, nor to the special adjustment problems involved in living in a white-dominated world. Instead of training teachers in new methods for helping youth of all classes to work out these personality adjustment problems, the few such demonstration centers open to Negro teachers are too apt to use as subjects the children of faculty members of the college where the training school is located. The psychological in-breeding involved in preparing teachers by having them practice with professors' children may remove the teacher still farther from the realities of her future job and make her even more impatient with the lower-class traits of the children with whom she has to deal later.

To give the teacher, the social worker, and the religious worker insight, patience, and ingenuity sufficient to coordinate community efforts for those youth who are most in need of new incentives is the final purpose of the demonstration projects.

NOT BY WAY OF SUMMARY

NOT BY WAY OF SUMMARY

EACH OF the three preceding chapters has explored all too briefly the need for improvement in the conditions affecting the personality development of Negro youth. Since these chapters are themselves an abridged analysis, there is no point at the close of the book in summarizing a summary. The reader is now merely reminded that as Negro youth face multiple limitations, improvement of their status must follow many lines of action.

The habit of thinking about Negroes as inferior, subordinate, and undeserving needs to be altered. Their right as persons to the good things of life must be increasingly taken for granted. Altering the stereotypes about Negroes will only come, however, when other people cease thinking and talking about them in the mass and begin to look at them as individuals.

Not only do Negro youth as persons deserve the right for fuller recognition, but for the sake of our democracy itself, their participation in the life of the nation is essential. Since internal unity and cooperation are as much a part of national defense as our battleships and fortifications, the importance of allowing no large minority to feel arbitrarily excluded is obvious. Equally obvious is the fact that during either peace or war, our democracy cannot stand by its principles if it practices within its boundaries what it condemns in other nations. Our handling of the race relations problem may well become a barometer measuring the efficiency with which our democratic principles may be put into practice.

Although developing new concepts concerning their place in the nation is a basic need of this minority group, Negro youth also have other urgent problems. How are they to continue their education? Where are they to find a job? When are they to be promoted? In what kind of a house are they to rear a family? What playgrounds are their children to use? These are homely questions, but they are vital concerns in the experience of Negro youth.

In addition to these crude and apparent needs, there are also other problems just as urgent but more subtle—problems for which educators, religious workers, and social workers have a special responsibility. These workers, representatives of a way of living which our society has approved, can influence the personality development of Negro youth if they understand the forces now at work and skillfully alter their course. They are the ones who in subtle ways can provide the rewards and incentives which will free many Negro children from one way of life and encourage them in another. They can break the cycle of adverse influences which have prevented some Negro youth from taking advantage of the opportunities which are already open to them.

To accomplish these ends, many specific suggestions were made, some having to do with the influence of public opinion, some having to do with the invention and spread of new patterns of race relations. Some recommendations were concerned with the special responsibilities of government; others with the example-setting responsibilities borne by large corporations, labor unions, patriotic, religious, and civic groups, and by communities where the racial problems are not acute. A project by which the findings of these and similar studies could be brought to bear upon trends in education, religion, and social welfare was outlined in some detail. The need for special courses in professional schools was also stressed.

Finally, all may agree that in meeting the Negro youth problem, as in dealing with other needs in our democratic life, there are two essential elements: the first consists of acquiring the correct *concepts,* and the second of developing the appropriate *procedures.* The place and possibilities of Negro youth in our democracy must be clearly conceived, and the improvement of their life according to these concepts must be carefully planned. No leader in American life can escape the responsibility of understanding how a tenth of the nation's youth lives and of helping to improve their way of living in keeping with our common ideals.

Photograph on jacket from Pictures Incorporated
Frontispiece by Lee, Farm Security Administration
Photograph facing page 24 from Howard University
Photograph facing page 25 from Howard University
Photograph facing page 40 by Post, Farm Security Administration
Photograph facing page 41 by Delano, Farm Security Administration
Photograph facing page 104 by Lee, Farm Security Administration
Photograph facing page 105 from Hampton Institute
Photograph facing page 120 from Hampton Institute
Photograph facing page 121 by Lee, Farm Security Administration

THE AMERICAN COUNCIL ON EDUCATION

GEORGE F. ZOOK, *President*

The American Council on Education is a *council* of national educational associations; organizations having related interests; approved universities and colleges, technological schools, and private secondary schools; state departments of education; and city school systems. It is a center of cooperation and coordination whose influence has been apparent in the shaping of American educational policies as well as in the formulation of American educational practices during the past twenty years. Many leaders in American education and public life serve on the commissions and committees through which the Council operates.

Established by the Council in 1935, the American Youth Commission consists of the persons whose names appear on a front page of this publication. It operates through a staff under the supervision and control of a director responsible to the Commission.